The Friends of Voltaire

Evelyn Beatrice Hall
(Under the pen name "S. G. Tallentyre")

Original publication: LONDON: SMITH, ELDER, & CO., 15 WATERLOO PLACE, 1906

ISBN: 9781980332558
Cover: Jean Huber, *Un dîner de philosophes.*

'Il faut que les âmes pensantes se frottent l'une contre l'autre pour fairs jaillir de la lumière.'
VOLTAIRE: *Letter to the Duc d'Uzès, December 4, 1751.*

CONTENTS

CONTENTS..5
Some Sources of Information................................7
I: D'ALEMBERT: THE THINKER.........................9
II: DIDEROT: THE TALKER................................25
III: GALIANI: THE WIT......................................41
IV: VAUVENARGUES: THE APHORIST.............59
V: D'HOLBACH: THE HOST..............................70
VI: GRIMM: THE JOURNALIST........................87
VII: HELVÉTIUS: THE CONTRADICTION.......101
VIII: TURGOT: THE STATESMAN....................117
IX: BEAUMARCHAIS: THE PLAYWRIGHT......133
X: CONDORCET: THE ARISTOCRAT..............150

Some Sources of Information

D'Alembert. *Joseph Bertrand.*
Œuvres et Correspondance inédites. *D'Alembert.*
Correspondance avec d'Alembert. *Marquise du Deffand.*
Diderot and the Encyclopædists. *John Morley.*
Éloge de d'Alembert. *Condorcet.*
Œuvres. *Diderot.*
Diderot. *Reinach.*
Diderot, l'Homme et l'Ecrivain. *Ducros.*
Diderot. *Scherer.*
Diderot et Catherine II. *Tourneux.*
Ferdinando Galiani, Correspondance, Étude, etc. *Perrey et Maugras.*
Lettres de l'Abbé Galiani. *Eugene Asse.*
Mémoires et Correspondance. *Madame d'Épinay.*
Jeunesse de Madame d'Épinay. *Perrey et Maugras.*
Dernières Années de Madame d'Épinay. *Perrey et Maugras.*
Mémoires. *Marmontel.*
Mémoires. *Morellet.*
Causeries du Lundi. *Sainte-Beuve.*
Vauvenargues. *Paléologue.*
Œuvres et Éloge de Vauvenargues. *D. L. Gilbert.*
Melchior Grimm. *Scherer.*
Rousseau. *John. Morley.*
Miscellanies. *John Morley.*
Correspondance Littéraire. *Grimm et Diderot.*
Turgot. *Léon Say.*
Turgot. *W. B. Hodgson.*
Œuvres. *Turgot.*
Vie de Turgot. *Condorcet.*
Correspondance inédite de Condorcet et Turgot. *C. Henry.*
La Marquise de Condorcet. *Guillois.*
Vie de Condorcet. *Robinet.*
Beaumarchais et Son Temps. *Loménie.*
Beaumarchais. *Hallays.*
Théâtre de Beaumarchais.
La Fin de l'Ancien Regime. *Imbert de Saint-Amand.*
French Revolution. *Carlyle.*
Critical Essays. *Carlyle.*
Correspondance. *Voltaire.*
Portraits Littéraires du XVIIIe Siecle. *La Harpe.*

Cours de Littérature. *La Harpe.*
Mémoire sur Helvétius. *Damiron.*
Le Salon de Madame Helvétius. *Guillois.*
Histoire de la Philosophie Moderne. *Buhle.*
Life of Hume. *Burton.*
The Private Correspondence of Garrick with Celebrated Persons.
Mémoires pour servir a l'Histoire de la Philosophie. *Damiron.*
Letters. *Laurence Sterne.*

I: D'ALEMBERT: THE THINKER

Of that vast intellectual movement which prepared the way for the most famous event in history, the French Revolution, Voltaire was the creative spirit.
But there was a group of men, less famous but not less great, who also heralded the coming of the new heaven and the new earth; who were in a strict sense friends and fellow-workers of Voltaire, although one or two of them were personally little known to him; whose aim was his aim, to destroy from among the people 'ignorance, the curse of God,' and who were, as he was, the prophets and the makers of a new dispensation.
That many of these light bringers were themselves full of darkness, is true enough; but they brought the light not the less, and in their own breasts burnt one cleansing flame, the passion for humanity.
For the rest, they were the typical men of the most enthralling age in history—each with his human story as well as his public purpose, and his part to play on the glittering stage of the social life of old France, as well as in the great events which moulded her destiny and affected the fate of Europe.

* * *

Foremost among them was d'Alembert.
Often talked about but little known, or vaguely remembered only as the patient lover of Mademoiselle de Lespinasse, Jean Lerond d'Alembert, the successor of Newton, the author of the Preface of the Encyclopædia, deserves an enduring fame.
On a November evening in the year 1717, one hundred and eighty-nine years ago, a *gendarme*, going his round in Paris, discovered on the steps of the church of Saint-Jean Lerond, once the baptistery of Notre-Dame, a child of a few hours old. The story runs that the baby was richly clad, and had on his small person marks which would lead to his identification. But the fact remains that he was abandoned in mid-winter, left without food or shelter to take his feeble chance of life and of the cold charity of some such institution as the Enfants Trouvés. It was no thanks to the mother who bore him that the *gendarme* who found him had compassion on his helpless infancy. The man had the baby hurriedly christened after his first cradle, Jean Baptiste Lerond, took him to a working woman whom he could trust, and who nursed him—for six weeks say some authorities, for a few days say others—in the little village of Crémery near Montdidier.

At the end of the time there returned to Paris a certain gallant General Destouches, who had been abroad in the execution of his military duties. He went to visit Madame de Tencin, and from her learnt of the birth and the abandonment of their son. No study of the eighteenth century can be complete without mention of the extraordinary women who were born with that marvellous age, and fortunately died with it. Cold, calculating, and corrupt, with the devilish cleverness of a Machiavelli, with the natural instinct of love used for gain and for trickery, and with the natural instinct of maternity wholly absent, d'Alembert's mother was the most perfect type of this monstrous class. Small, keen, alert, with a little sharp face like a bird's, brilliantly eloquent, bold, subtle, tireless, a great minister of intrigue, and insatiably ambitious—such was Madame de Tencin. It was she who assisted at the meetings of statesmen, and gave Marshal Richelieu a plan and a line of conduct. It was she who managed the affairs of her brother Cardinal de Tencin, and, through him, tried to effect peace between France and Frederick in the midst of the Seven Years' War. It was she who fought the hideous incompetence of Maurepas, the Naval Minister; and it was she who summed herself up to Fontenelle when she laid her hand on her heart, saying, 'Here is nothing but brain.'

From the moment of his birth she had only one wish with regard to her child—to be rid of him. A long procession of lovers had left her wholly incapable of shame. But the child would be a worry—and she did not mean to be worried! If the father had better instincts—well, let him follow them. He did. He employed Molin, Madame de Tencin's doctor, to find out the baby's nurse, Anne Lemaire, and claim the little creature from her.

The great d'Alembert told Madame Suard many years after how Destouches drove all round Paris with the baby ('with a head no bigger than an apple') in his arms, trying to find for him a suitable foster-mother. But little Jean Baptiste Lerond seemed to be dying, and no one would take him. At last, however, Destouches discovered, living in the Rue Michel-Lecomte, a poor glazier's wife, whose motherly soul was touched by the infant's piteous plight, and who took him to her love and care, and kept him there for fifty years.

History has concerned itself much less with Madame Rousseau than with Madame de Tencin. Yet it was the glazier's wife who was d'Alembert's real mother after all. If she was low-born and ignorant, she had yet the happiest of all acquirements—she knew how to win love and to keep it. The great d'Alembert, universally acclaimed as one of the first intellects of Europe, had ever for this simple person, who defined a philosopher as 'a fool who torments himself during his life that people may talk of him when he is dead,' the tender reverence which true greatness, and only true greatness perhaps, can bear towards homely goodness. From her he learnt the blessing of peace and obscurity. From his association with her he learnt his noble idea—difficult in any age, but in that age of degrading luxury and self-indulgence well nigh impossible—that it is sinful to enjoy superfluities while other men want necessaries. His hidden life in the dark attic above her husband's shop made it possible for him to do that life's work. For nearly half a century he knew no other home. When he left her roof at last, in obedience to the voice of the most masterful of all human passions, he still retained for her the tenderest affection, and bestowed upon her and her grandchildren the kindness of one of the kindest hearts that ever beautified a great intelligence.

Little Jean Baptiste was put to a school in the Faubourg Saint-Antoine, where he passed as Madame Rousseau's son. General Destouches paid the expenses of this schooling, took a keen pleasure in the child's brightness and precocity, and came often to see him. One day he persuaded Madame de Tencin to accompany him. The seven-year-old Jean Baptiste remembered that scene all his life. 'Confess, Madame,' says Destouches, when they had listened to the boy's clever answers to his master's questions, 'that it was a pity to abandon such a child.' Madame rose at once. 'Let us go. I see it is going to be very uncomfortable for me here.' She never came again.

Destouches died in 1726, when his son was nine years old. He left the boy twelve hundred livres, and commended him to the care of his relatives. Through them, at the age of twelve, Jean Baptiste received the great favour of being admitted to the College of the Four Nations, founded by Mazarin, and in 1729 the most exclusive school in France. Fortunately for its new scholar it was something besides fashionable, and did its best to satisfy his extraordinary thirst for knowledge. His teachers were all priests and Jansenists, and nourished their apt scholar on Jansenist literature, imbuing him with the fashionable theories of Descartes. How soon was it that they began to hope and dream that in the gentle student called Lerond, living on a narrow pittance above a tradesman's shop, they

had found a new Pascal, a mighty enemy of the Archfiend Jesuitism?
But beneath his timid and modest exterior there lay already an intellect of marvellous strength and clearness, a relentless logic that tested and weighed every principle instilled in him, every theory masquerading as a fact. He quickly became equally hostile to both Jesuit and Jansenist. It was at school that he learnt to hate with an undying hatred, religion—the religion that in forty years launched, on account of the Bull Unigenitus, forty thousand *lettres de cachet*, that made men forget not only their Christianity but their humanity, and give themselves over body and soul to the devouring fever called fanaticism. At school also he conceived his passion for mathematics, that love of exact truth which no Jansenist priest, however subtle, could make him regard as a dangerous error. When he was eighteen, in 1735, he took his degree of Bachelor of Arts and changed his name. D'Alembert is thought to be an anagram on Baptiste Lerond. Anagrams were fashionable, and one Arouet, who had elected to be called Voltaire, had made such an alteration of good omen. D'Alembert went on studying at the College, but throughout his studies mathematics were wooing him from all other pursuits. The taste, however, was so unlucrative, and the income from twelve hundred livres so small, that a profession became a necessity. The young man conscientiously qualified for a barrister. But 'he loved only good causes' and was naturally shy. He never appeared at the Bar. Then he bethought him of medicine. He would be a doctor! But again and again the siren voice of his dominant taste called him back to her. His friends —those omniscient friends always ready to put a spoke in the wheel of genius—entreated him to be practical, to remember his poverty, and to make haste to grow rich. He yielded to them so far that one day he carried all his geometrical books to one of their houses, and went back to the garret at Madame Rousseau's to study medicine and nothing else in the world. But the geometrical problems disturbed his sleep.
  —One master-passion in the breast,
  Like Aaron's serpent, swallowed all the rest.

Fate wanted d'Alembert, the great mathematician, not some prosperous, unproductive mediocrity of a Paris apothecary. The crowning blessing of life, to be born with a bias to some pursuit, was this man's to the full.
He yielded to Nature and to God. He brought back the books

I: D'ALEMBERT: THE THINKER

he had abandoned, flung aside those for which he had neither taste nor aptitude, and at twenty gave himself to the work for which he had been created.

Some artist should put on canvas the picture of this student, sitting in his ill-aired garret with its narrow prospect of 'three ells of sky,' poor, delicate, obscure—or rich, rather, in the purest of earthly enjoyments, the pursuit of truth for its own sake. He could not afford to buy many of the books he needed, so he borrowed them from public libraries. He left the work of the day anticipating with joy the work of the morrow. For the world he cared nothing, and of him it knew nothing. Fame?—he did not want it. Wealth?—he could do without it. Poor as he was, there was no time when he even thought of taking pupils, or using the leisure he needed for study in making money by a professorship.

To give knowledge was his work and his aim; to make knowledge easier for others he left to some lesser man. His style had seldom the grace and clearness which can make, and which in many of his fellow-workers did make, the abstrusest reasoning charm like romance. D'Alembert left Diderot to put his thought into irresistible words, and Voltaire and Turgot to translate it into immortal deeds.

When he was two-and-twenty, in 1739, d'Alembert began his connection with the Academy of Sciences. In 1743 he published his 'Treatise on Dynamics.' Now little read and long superseded, it placed him at one bound, and at six-and-twenty years old, among the first geometricians of Europe. Modest, frugal, retiring as he was and remained, he was no more only the loving and patient disciple of science. He was its master and teacher. In 1746 his 'Treatise on the Theory of Winds' gained him a prize in the Academy of Berlin, and first brought him into relationship with Frederick the Great.

Two years later, when her son was of daily growing renown, Madame de Tencin died. The story that, when he had become famous and she would fain have acknowledged him, he had repudiated her, saying he had no mother but the glazier's wife, d'Alembert, declares Madame Suard, always denied. 'I should never have refused her endearments—it would have been too sweet to me to recover her.' That answer is more in keeping with a temperament but too gentle and forgiving, than the spirited repulse. It was in keeping also with the life of Madame de Tencin that even death should leave her indifferent to her child. She thought no more of him, he said, in the one than in the other. Her money she left to her doctor.

If the studious poverty of the life in the glazier's attic spared d'Alembert acquaintances, it did not deprive him of friends. Then living in Paris, some six-and-thirty years old, the author of the 'Philosophical Thoughts,' and the most fascinating scoundrel in France, was Denis Diderot. With the quiet d'Alembert, of morals almost austere and of hidden, frugal life, what could a Diderot have in common? Something more than the attraction of opposites drew them together. The vehement and all-embracing imagination of the one fired the calm reason of the other. The hot head and the cool one were laid together, and the result was the great Encyclopædia. The first idea of the pair was modest enough—to translate into French the English Encyclopædia of Chambers. But had not brother Voltaire said that no man who could make an adequate translation ever wasted his time in translating? They soon out-ran so timid an ambition. The thing must not only be spontaneous work; it must wholly surpass all its patterns and prototypes. It must be not an Encyclopædia, but *the* Encyclopædia. Every man of talent in France must bring a stone towards the building of the great Temple. From Switzerland, old Voltaire shall pour forth inspiration, encouragement, incentive. Rousseau shall lend it the glow of his passion, and Grimm his journalistic versatility. Helvétius shall contribute—d'Holbach, Turgot, Morellet, Marmontel, Raynal, La Harpe, de Jaucourt, Duclos.
And the Preliminary Discourse shall be the work of d'Alembert.
An envious enemy once dismissed him scornfully as
—Chancelier de Parnasse,
Qui se croit un grand homme et fit une préface.

Yet if he had written nothing but that Preface he would still have had noble titles to fame. It contained, as he himself said, the quintessence of twenty years' study. If his style was usually cold and formal, it was not so now. With warmest eloquence and boldest brush he painted the picture of the progress of the human mind since the invention of printing. From the lofty heights man's intellect had scaled there stood out yet mightier heights for him to dare! Advance! advance! If ever preface said anything, the Preface to the great Encyclopædia says this. Clothed with light and fire, that dearest son of d'Alembert's genius went forth to illuminate and to astound the world.
At first the Encyclopædia was not only heard gladly by the

I: D'ALEMBERT: THE THINKER

common people, but was splendidly set forth with the approbation and *Privilège du Roi*. Even the wise and thoughtful melancholy of d'Alembert's temperament may have been cheered by such good fortune, while the sanguine Diderot naturally felt convinced it would last for ever.
Both worked unremittingly. His authorship of the Preface immediately flung open to d'Alembert all the *salons* in Paris, and for the first time in his life he began to go into society. Then Frederick the Great made him a rich and splendid offer, the Presidency of the Berlin Academy. Consider that though the man was famous he was still very poor. The little pension which was his all 'is hardly enough to keep me if I have the happiness or the misfortune to live to be old.' From the Government of his country he feared everything and hoped nothing. He was only thirty-five years of age. A new world was opened to him. The glazier's attic he could exchange for a palace, and the homely kindness of an illiterate foster-mother for the magnificent endearments of a philosophic king. Was it only the painful example of friend Voltaire's angry wretchedness as Frederick's guest that made him refuse an offer so lavish and so dazzling? It was rather that he had the rare wisdom to recognise happiness when he had it and did not mistake it for some phantom will-o'-the-wisp whom distance clothed with light. 'The peace I enjoy is so perfect,' he wrote, 'I dare run no risk of disturbing it. ... I do not doubt the King's goodness ... only that the conditions essential to happiness are not in his power.'
Any man who is offered in place of quiet content that most fleeting and unsubstantial of all chimeras—fame and glory— should read d'Alembert's answer to Frederick the Great. Frederick's royal response to it was the offer of a pension of twelve hundred livres.
In September 1754 the fourth volume of the Encyclopædia was hailed by the world with a burst of enthusiasm and applause, and in the December of that year d'Alembert received as a reward for his indefatigable labours a chair in the French Academy. He had only accepted it on condition that he spoke his mind freely on all points and made court to no man. The speech with which he took his seat, though constantly interrupted with clapping and cries of delight, was not good, said Grimm. All d'Alembert's addresses and *éloges* spoken at the Academy leave posterity, indeed, as cold as they left the astute German journalist. The man was a mathematician, a creature of reason. The passion that was to rule that reason

and dominate his life was not the gaudy and shallow passion of the orator.

In 1756 he went to stay with the great head of his party, Voltaire, at the Délices, near Geneva. The Patriarch was sixty-two years old, but with the activity and the enthusiasm of youth. At his house and at his table d'Alembert met constantly and observed deeply the Calvinistic pastors of Geneva. He returned to Paris with his head full of the most famous article the Encyclopædia was to know. At the back of his mind was a certain request of his host's, that he should also make a few remarks on the benefits that play-acting would confer on the Calvinistic temperament.

No article in that 'huge folio dictionary' brewed so fierce a storm or had consequences so memorable and far-reaching as d'Alembert's article 'Geneva.' In his reserved and formal style he punctiliously complimented the descendants of Calvin as preferring reason to faith, sound sense to dogma, and as having a religion which, weighed and tested, was nothing but a perfect Socinianism. Voltaire laughed long in his sleeve, and in private executed moral capers of delight. The few words on the advantages of play-acting, which he had begged might be added, had not been forgotten.

The Genevan pastors took solemn and heartburning counsel together, and on the head of the quiet worker in the attic in Paris there burst a hurricane which might have beaten down coarser natures and frightened stouter hearts. Calvinism fell upon him, whose sole crime had been to show her the logical outcome of her doctrines, with the fierce fury of a desperate cause. Retract! retract! or at least give the names of those of our pastors who made you believe in the rationalism of our creed! As for the remarks on plays, why, Jean Jacques Rousseau, our citizen and your brother philosopher, shall answer those, and in the dazzling rhetoric of the immortal 'Letter on Plays' give, with all the magic and enchantment of his sophist's genius, the case against the theatre.

Then, on March 8, 1759, the paternal government of France, joining hands with Geneva, suppressed by royal edict that Encyclopædia of which a very few years earlier it had solemnly approved. The accursed thing was burnt by the hangman. The printers and publishers were sent to the galleys or to death. The permit to continue publishing the work was rescinded. The full flowing fountain of knowledge was dammed, and the self-denial of d'Alembert's patient life wasted. The gentle heart, which had never harmed living

I: D'ALEMBERT: THE THINKER

creature, fell stricken beneath the torrent of filthy fury which the gutter press poured upon him. His Majesty—his besotted Majesty, King Louis the Fifteenth—finds in the Encyclopædia, forsooth, 'maxims tending to destroy Royal authority and to establish independence … corruption of morals, irreligion, and unbelief.' Sycophant and toadying Paris went with him. Furious and blaspheming, passionate Diderot came out to meet the foe. Dancing with rage, old Voltaire at Délices could only calm himself enough to hold a pen in his shaking fingers and pour out incentives to his brothers in Paris to fight till the death. To him injustice was ever the bugle-call to battle. But not to d'Alembert. He shrank back into his shell, dumb and wounded. 'I do not know if the Encyclopædia will be continued,' he wrote, 'but I am sure it will not be continued by me.' Even the stirring incitements of his chief could not alter his purpose. He had offered sight to the blind, and they had chosen darkness; he would bring them the light no more. That Diderot considered him traitor and apostate did not move him. He would not quarrel with that affectionate, hot-headed brother worker, but for himself that chapter of his life was finished, and he turned the page.

In the very same year he gave to a thankless world his 'Elements of Philosophy;' and he again refused Frederick the Great's invitation to exchange persecuting Paris for the Presidency of the Berlin Academy. But there was no reason why he should not escape from his troubles for a time and become Frederick's visitor.

In 1762 he went to Berlin for two months, and found the great King a clever, generous, and devoted friend. But though he continued to beg d'Alembert to stay with him permanently, and was lavish of gifts and promises, the wise and judicious visitor was wholly proof against the royal blandishments. In the same year he refused a yet more dazzling offer—to be tutor to Catherine the Great's son. He had already in Paris, not only ties, which might be broken, but a tie, which he found indissoluble.

In 1765, three years after Catherine's offer had been made and declined, d'Alembert, when he was forty-eight years old, was attacked by a severe illness, which, said his accommodating doctor, required larger and airier rooms than those in his good old nurse's home. He was moved from the familiar Rue Michel-Lecomte to the Boulevard du Temple. There Mademoiselle de Lespinasse joined him and nursed him back to health.

In all the story of d'Alembert's life, in that age of unbridled licence, no woman's name is connected with his save this one's. Fifteen years earlier he had made the acquaintance of Madame du Deffand. To the blind old worldling, who loved Horace Walpole and wrote immortal letters, he stood in the nature of a dear and promising son. For many years he was always about her house. His wit and his charm, seasoned by a gentle spice of irony and a delightful talent for telling stories and enjoying them himself, naturally endeared him to the old woman whose one hell was boredom. On his side, he came because he liked her, and stayed because he loved Mademoiselle de Lespinasse. The history of that *ménage*, of the brilliant, impulsive, undisciplined girl, with her plain face and her matchless charm, and of the blind old woman she tended, deceived, and outwitted, has been told in fiction as well as in history. How when Madame du Deffand was asleep, her poor companion held for herself reunions of the bright, particular stars of her mistress's firmament, and how the old woman, rising a little too early one day, came into the room and with her sightless eyes saw all, is one of the familiar anecdotes of literature.

Long before this dramatic *dénouement*, d'Alembert and Julie de Lespinasse had been something more than friends. But now Mademoiselle saw herself cast adrift on the world. She flung to it her reputation, and yielded, not so much to the entreaties of d'Alembert's love, as to the more pitiful pleading his solitude and sickness made to the warm maternity in her woman's heart. She nursed him back to convalescence, and then lived beneath the same roof with him in the Rue Belle Chasse.

Picture the man with his wide, wise intelligence and his diffident and gentle nature, and the woman with her brilliant intuition and her quick, glowing impulse. To his exact logic she could add feeling, passion, sympathy; his frigid and awkward style she could endow with life and fire. Many of his manuscripts are covered with her handwriting. Some, she certainly inspired. She had read widely and felt keenly, and her lover had weighed, pondered, considered. For him, who had for himself no ambition, she could dare and hope all. The perpetual Secretaryship of the Academy shall be turned from a dream to a fact! In that age of women's influence no woman had in her frail hands more to give and to withhold than this poor companion, whose marvellous power over men and destinies lay not in her head, but in her heart. The true complement of a d'Alembert, daring where he was timid, fervent where he was cold, a woman's feeling to quicken his man's reason—here should have been indeed the marriage of true minds.

> Oh, I must feel your brain prompt mine,
> Your heart anticipate my heart.
> You must be just before, in fine,
> See and make me see, for your part,
> New depths of the divine!

Yet d'Alembert's is the most piteous love-story in history. If Mademoiselle had yielded to his sadness and his loneliness, she had never loved him. Only a year after she had joined him, d'Alembert, alluding to some rumours which had been afloat concerning their marriage, wrote bitterly, 'What should I do with a wife and children?' But there was only one real obstacle to their union. Across Mademoiselle's undisciplined heart there lay already the shadows of another passion.
From the first the household in the Rue Belle Chasse had been absolutely dominated by the woman. 'In love, who loves least, rules.' D'Alembert was in bondage while she was free. To keep her, he submitted to humours full of bitterness and sharpness—the caprices of that indifferent affection which gives nothing and exacts all. In her hands, he was as a child; his philosophies went to the winds; his very reason was prostrate. How soon was it he began to guess he had a rival in her heart?
It was not till after her death that he found out for certain that less than two years after she came to him she had given herself, body and soul, to the young Marquis de Mora. But what he did not know, he must have greatly suspected. It was he who wrote her letters and ran her errands. Grimm recorded in the 'Literary Correspondence' the prodigious ascendency she had acquired over all his thoughts and actions. 'No luckless Savoyard of Paris ... does so many wearisome commissions as the first geometrician of Europe, the chief of the Encyclopædic sect, the dictator of our Academies, does for Mademoiselle.' He would post her fervent outpourings to the man who had supplanted him, and call for the replies at the post-office that she might receive them an hour or two earlier. What wonder that over such a character, a nature like Mademoiselle's rode roughshod, that she hurt and bruised him a hundred times a day, and wounded while she despised him? No woman ever truly loves a man who does not exact

from her not only complete fidelity to himself, but fidelity to all that is best and highest in her own nature.

D'Alembert had indeed in full measure the virtue of his defects. If it was a crime to be tender to her sins, it was nobility to be gentle to her sufferings. He bore and forbore with her endlessly. Always patient and good-humoured, thinking greatly of her and little of himself, abundant in compassion for her ruined nerves and the querulous feverishness of her ill health—here surely were some of the noble traits of a good love. He read to her, watched by her, tended her, and in the matchless society they gathered round them was abundantly content to be nothing, that she might be all.

Their life together in the Rue Belle Chase had not in the least shocked their easy-going world. Many persons comfortably maintained that their association was the merest friendship—heedless of that amply proven fact that where people avoid evil, they avoid also the appearance of evil. The eighteenth century, indeed, even if it saw any difference between vice and virtue, which is doubtful, did not in the least mind if its favourites were vicious or virtuous, provided they were not dull. D'Alembert and Mademoiselle de Lespinasse did not fall under that ban. The hermit life the man had led was over for ever. In her modest room in that dingy street. Mademoiselle held every night the most famous *salon* in Paris.

Most of the *salons* may be exhaustively described as having been nourished on a little *eau sucré* and a great deal of wit. But to this one wit alone was light, food, and air. Mademoiselle did not require to give dinners like Madame Necker, or suppers like Madame du Deffand; neither for the beauty which, later, was to make men forgive the mental limitations of Madame Recámier, had she need or use. Tall, pale, and slender, with her infinite, unconscious tact, her mental grace, and her divine sympathy, her passage through the social life of her age has left the subtle perfume of some delicate flower. To be her friend was to feel complete, understood, satisfied. To her, as to a sister of consolation, came Condorcet, marquis, mathematician, philosopher; Saint-Pierre, the pupil of Rousseau and the creator of 'Paul and Virginia;' La Harpe, whom she was to help to the Academy; Hénault, whom she had charmed from Madame du Deffand; Turgot, Chastellux, Marmontel. And quietly effacing himself, with that true greatness which is never afraid to be made of little account, was Mademoiselle's lover and the noblest intellect of them all, d'Alembert.

I: D'ALEMBERT: THE THINKER

There is no more delightful trait in his character than this exquisite talent for modesty. With his spare form always dressed from head to foot in clothes of one colour, the aim of d'Alembert was both physically and mentally, as it were, to escape notice. True, when he talked, the listener must needs marvel at the breadth, the variety, the exhaustless interests of the mind, and its perfect simplicity and straightforwardness. But he did not want to talk much. He liked better to listen. He preferred in society, as he preferred in life, to think while other men said and did.

No social pleasures could either supersede the work of his life, or make compensation for the sorrows of his soul. He had already thrown in his lot with Mademoiselle when he published the most daring of all his books, 'The History of the Destruction of the Jesuits.' Her treachery had shattered his life for five years, when he asked Frederick the Great for a sum of money which would enable him to travel and heal his broken health and heart. In 1770, with young Condorcet for his companion, he left Paris for Italy, stopped at Ferney, and spent his whole leave of absence with Voltaire.

It was an oasis in the desert of the feverish existence to which he had condemned himself. In mighty speculation, in splendid visions of the future of the race, in passionate argument on the immortality of the soul and the being and nature of God, he forgot his personal sorrows. The mind dominated and the heart was still. What nights the three must have spent together —Voltaire with his octogenarian's intellect as keen and bright as a boy's, the young Marquis, sharp-set to learn, and d'Alembert with his 'just mind and inexhaustible imagination'—when they could get rid of that babbling inconsequence, Voltaire's niece, Madame Denis, and sit hour after hour discussing, planning, dreaming! The quiet d'Alembert went, as quiet people often do, far beyond his impulsive and outspoken companions in speculative daring. Though there is not an anti-Christian line in any of his published writings except his correspondence, yet the scepticism of this gentle mathematician far exceeded that of him who is accounted the Prince of Unbelievers, and where his host was a hotly convinced Deist, d'Alembert only thought the probabilities in favour of Theism, and was far more Voltairian than Voltaire. It was the old Pontiff of the Church of Anti-Christ who stopped a conversation at his table wherein d'Alembert had spoken of the very existence of God as a moot point, by sending the servants out of the room, and then turning to his guests with—'And now, gentlemen, continue your attack upon God. But as I do not want to be murdered or robbed to-night by my servants, they had better not hear you.' The visit lasted in all two months. D'Alembert abandoned the Italian journey, offered King Frederick his change, and returned to Paris.

In 1772 he was made Perpetual Secretary of the French Academy. He, whose needs, said Grimm, were always the measure of his ambitions, had scaled heights, not beyond his deserts, but beyond his wishes. He was also a member of the scientific Academies of Prussia, Russia, Portugal, Naples, Turin, Norway, Padua, and of the literary academies of Sweden and Bologna. But if 'the end of an ambition is to be happy at home,' d'Alembert had failed. When the Perpetual Secretaryship was still a new and dazzling possession, the Perpetual Secretary found at home the woman to whom he was captive soul and body, in the throes of another passion. False to de Mora, as she had been false to him, she was then writing to de Guibert those love-letters which have given her a place beside Sappho and Eloïsa and have added a classic to literature. It was d'Alembert's part to listen to self-reproaches whose justice he might well guess, to look into the depths of a tenderness in which he had no share. Once he gave her his portrait with these lines beneath it:

> Et dites quelquefois en voyant cette image
> De tous ceux que j'aimai, qui m'aima comme lui?

She herself said that of all the feelings she had inspired, his alone had not brought her wretchedness.

In 1775 de Guibert was married. The marriage was Mademoiselle's death-blow. The fever of the soul became a disease of the body. Sometimes bitterly repentant and sometimes only captious and difficult; now, her true self full of tenderness and charm: and now, reckless, selfish, despairing—d'Alembert's patience and goodness were inexhaustible. True to his character, he stood aside that to the last her friends might visit her, that to the last she might help and feel for them.

But though the spirit still triumphed at moments over the body, the end was near. When her misery was dulled by opium, d'Alembert was always watching, unheeded, at her bedside. It was the attitude of his life. When she became conscious, he was there still. Before she died, she asked his pardon; but de Guibert's was the last name upon her lips. She

I: D'ALEMBERT: THE THINKER

died on May 23, 1776, not yet forty-five years old.
D'Alembert's grief seems to have taken by surprise many short-sighted friends who had supposed that quiet exterior to hide a cold, or an unawakened, heart. He was utterly crushed and broken. His life had lost at once its inspiration and its meaning. For the sake of Mademoiselle he had grown old without family and without hope. His friends, in that age of noble friendships, did their best to comfort him. But his wounds were deeper than they knew. With a super-refinement of selfishness or cruelty, Mademoiselle had left him her Correspondence. She had not preserved in it one single line of the many letters he had himself written to her, while it contained full and certain proofs of her double infidelity.
He who has lost only those of whose faith and truth he is sure, has not yet reached the depth of human desolation.
After a while, d'Alembert tried to return to his first affection—that cold but faithful mistress, his mathematical studies. At the Academy he pronounced the *éloge* of Louis de Sacy, who had been the lover of the Marquise de Lambert. For the first time he looked into his heart and wrote, and thus for the first time he touched the hearts of others; the cold style took fire, and beneath the clumsy periods welled tears.
But the writer was consumed to the soul with grief and weariness. This was not the man who could use sorrow as a spur to new endeavour and to nobler work. Before the persecutions which had assailed the Encyclopædia he had bowed his head and taken covert, and the death of his mistress broke not only his heart, but his spirit and his life. From Madame Marmontel and from Thomas, he derived, it is said, some sort of comfort: Condorcet was as a son; but with Mademoiselle's death the light of her society had gone out. The friends who remained were but pale stars in a dark sky. D'Alembert was growing old. He suffered from a cruel disease and could not face the horrors of the operation which might have relieved it. 'Those are fortunate who have courage,' said he; 'for myself, I have none.' It was life, not death, he dreaded. What use then to suffer only to prolong suffering?
The mental enlightenment he had given the world, the wider knowledge which he had lived to impart, consoled this dying thinker scarcely at all. He was to his last hour what he had been when Mademoiselle took ill-fated compassion on his dependence and loneliness—a child, affectionate, solitary, tractable, with the great mind always weighed down by the

supersensitiveness of a child's heart and with a child's clinging need of care and tenderness. He died on October 29, 1783.

The man whose only reason for dreading poverty had been lest he should be forced to reduce his charities, left, as might have been expected, a very small fortune. Condorcet was his residuary legatee, and made his *éloge* in both the Academies. Diderot himself was dying when he heard of his old friend's death. 'A great light has gone out,' said he. Euler, d'Alembert's brother, and sometimes his rival, geometrician, survived him only a few months. And Voltaire, the quick and life-giving spirit of the vast movement of which d'Alembert was the Logic, the Reason, the Thought, had already died to earth, though he lived to everlasting fame.

D'Alembert owes his greatest reputation to geometry. But, as Grimm said, in that department only geometricians can exactly render him his due: 'He added to the discoveries of the Eulers ... and the Newtons.' To the general public his great title to glory lies in the mighty help he gave to that great monument of Voltairian philosophy, the Encyclopædia. The Preface was 'a work for which he had no model.' By it, he introduced to the world that book which Diderot produced, and which, except the Bible and the Koran, may be justly said to have been the most influential book in history; which gave France, and, through France, Europe, that new light and knowledge which brought with them a nobler civilisation and a recognition of the universal rights of man.

In himself, d'Alembert was always rather a great intelligence than a great character. To the magnificence of the one he owed all that has made him immortal, and to the weakness of the other the sorrows and the failures of his life. For it is by character and not by intellect the world is won.

II: DIDEROT: THE TALKER

Some hundred and eighty odd years ago, in a little town in France, a wild boy slipped out of his room at midnight, and crept downstairs in his stocking-feet with the wicked intent of running away to Paris. This time-honoured escapade was defeated by the appearance of Master Denis's resolute father with the household keys in his hand. 'Where are you going?' says he. 'To Paris, to join the Jesuits.' 'Certainly; I will take you there myself to-morrow.' And Denis retires tamely and ignominiously to bed.

The next morning the good old father (a master-cutler in the town of Langres) escorted his scapegrace to the capital, as he had desired, entered him at Harcourt College, stayed himself for a fortnight at a neighbouring inn to see that the boy adhered to his intentions; and then went home. The adventure was redeemed from the commonplace in that this scapegrace would fain have run away, not *from* school, but *to* it; and that he was acting under an influence much more powerful than the cheap, adventurous fiction which generally prompts such schemes. When he was twelve years old the Jesuits had tonsured Denis's hot head, and no doubt designed all it contained for their service.

At the college Denis spent his time in learning a great deal for himself, and doing, with brilliant ease and the most complete good-nature, a great deal of work of his school-fellows. He was himself astoundingly clever and astoundingly careless. He learnt mathematics, which could not make him exact, Latin, and English. With that charming readiness to do the stupid boys' lessons for them (*blanchir les chiffons des autres*, the talent came to be called when he grew older), with his inimitable love of life, his jolly, happy-go-lucky disposition, his open hand and heart, and his merry face, this should surely have been the most popular schoolboy that ever lived. One of his friends was Bernis—to be poet, Cardinal, and *protégé* of Madame de Pompadour—and the pair would dine together at six sous a head at a neighbouring restaurant.

The schooldays were all too short. The practical master-cutler at Langres soon intimated to Denis that it was time to choose a profession. But Denis declines to be a doctor, because he has no turn for murder; or a lawyer, because he has no taste for doing other people's business. In brief, he does not want to be anything. He wants to learn, to study, to look round him. But a shrewd old tradesman is not going to give, even if he could afford to give, any son of his the money to do that. Denis had at home a younger brother, who was to be a priest ('that cursed saint,' the graceless Denis called him hereafter), a sister, good and sensible like her father, and a mother, who was tender and foolish over her truant boy, after the fashion of mothers all the world over. Here were three mouths to feed. Denis loved his father with all the impetuous affection of his temperament. He was delighted when, some years later, he went back to Langres and a fellow-townsman grasped him by the arm saying: 'M. Diderot, you are a good man, but if you think you will ever be as good a man as your father, you are much mistaken.' But Diderot had never the sort of affection that consists in doing one's utmost for the object of the affection. He preferred to be a care and a trouble to his family and to live by his wits, harum-scarum, merry, and poor. He chose that life, and abided by the choice for ten years.

Three times in that period the old servant of the family tramped all the way from Langres to Paris with little stores of money hidden in her dress for this dear, naughty scapegrace of a Master Denis; but except for this, he lived on his wits in the most literal sense of the term. He made catalogues and translations; he wrote sermons and thought himself well paid at fifty *écus* the homily; he became a tutor—until the pupil's stupidity bored him, when he threw up the situation and went hungry to bed. He once indeed so far commanded himself as to remain in this capacity for three months. Then he sought his employer; he could endure it no more. 'I am making men of your children, perhaps; but they are fast making a child of me. I am only too well off and comfortable in your house, but I must leave it.' And he left.

One Shrove Tuesday he fainted from hunger in his wretched lodgings, and was restored and fed by his landlady. He took a vow that day, and kept it, that, if he had anything to give, he would never refuse a man in need. By the next morning he was as light-hearted as usual again. A bright idea, even the recollection of a few apt lines from Horace, would always restore his cheerfulness. He enjoyed indeed all the blessings of a sanguine nature, and fell into all its faults. The facts that his father was paying his debts, that often he had to sponge on his friends for a dinner, or trick a tradesman for an advantage he could not buy, neither troubled him nor made him work. It is no doubt to his credit that he never stooped, as he might easily have done, to be the literary parasite of some great man, to prostitute his talents to praise and fawn on some ignoble patron. But though that gay, profligate existence has been often made to sound romantic on paper, it was squalid and shabby enough in reality, with that shabbiness which is of the soul.

In the year 1743, when Diderot was thirty years old, he must needs fall in love. He was lodging with a poor woman and her daughter who kept themselves by doing fine needlework. Anne Toinette Champion (Nanette, Diderot called her) was not only exquisitely fresh and pretty, but she was good, simple, and honest. To gain access to her Diderot stooped to one of the tricks to which his life had made him used. He pretended that he was going to enter a Jesuit seminary, and employed Nanette to make him the necessary outfit. His mouth of gold did the rest. No one, perhaps, who did not live with Diderot and hear him talk 'as never man talked,' who did not know him in the flesh and fall under the personal influence of his magnetic and all-compelling charm, will ever fully understand it. 'Utterly unclean, scandalous, shameless' as many honest and upright people knew him to be, he fascinated them all. Something indeed of that fascination still lingers about him, as the scent of a flower may cling to a coarse, stained parchment. Read the facts of his life, as briefly and coldly stated in some biographical dictionary, and most men will easily dismiss him as a great genius and a great scoundrel. Read the thousand anecdotes that have gathered about his name, of the love his contemporaries bore him, of his generosity, his glowing affections, his passionate pity for sorrow, and his hot zeal for humanity, and it is easy to understand not only the mighty part Diderot played in the great movement which prepared men for freedom and the French Revolution, but also his insistent claims on their love and forgiveness.

A little seamstress could not, in the nature of things, resist him long. The hopeful lover went to Langres to obtain his father's consent to his marriage, which was of course refused. At the date of his wedding, November 6, 1743, Denis had published scarcely anything, had no certain sources of income, and very few uncertain ones. He was, moreover, at first so jealous of his dearest Nanette that he made her give up her trade of needlework, as it brought her too much into contact with the outer world. The pair lived on her mother's savings; and then Denis translated a history of Greece from the English, and kept the wolf from the door a little longer.

Poverty fell, as ever, more hardly on the wife than on the husband. The ever popular Diderot was often asked out to dine with his friends, and always went; while at home Nanette feasted on dry bread, to be sure that this fine lover of hers should be able to have his cup of coffee and his game of chess at the *café* of the Regency as usual. Of course Denis took advantage of her talent for self-sacrifice. His writings contain much sentimental pity, expressed in the most beautiful language, for the condition and the physical disadvantages of women; and he spoke of himself most comfortably as a good husband and father, and honestly believed that he was both. But he began to neglect his wife directly his first passion for her was spent. She was not perfect, it is true. Of a certain rigidity in her goodness, and a certain bourgeois narrowness in her view of life, she may be justly accused. But it remains undeniable that she was thrifty and unselfish at home, while her husband was profligate and self-indulgent abroad, that she saved and worked for her children, while he wrote fine pages on paternal devotion, and that he never gave her the consideration and forbearance he demanded *from* her as a matter of course. Before her first child was born the poor girl had lost her mother, and had no one in all the world to depend on but that most untrustworthy creature on earth, a genius of bad character.

In the year 1745 Denis sent her to Langres for a long visit to his parents, to effect if possible a reconciliation with them. The man who called himself 'the apologist of strong passions,' who thought marriage 'a senseless vow,' and 'was always very near to the position that there is no such thing as an absolute rule of right and wrong,' would not be likely to be faithful. He was not faithful. There soon loomed on the scene a Madame Puisieux (the wife of a barrister), aged about five-and-twenty, charming, accomplished, dissolute. Diderot plunged headlong into love with her, as he plunged headlong into everything. To be sure, she was abominably extravagant and always wanting money. To gratify her demands Diderot wrote, most characteristically, an 'Essay on Merit and Virtue,' and brought Merit and Virtue the sum he received in payment. But Madame's love of fine clothes was insatiable. Between a Good Friday and Easter Day her lover composed for her the 'Philosophical Thoughts,' which first made him famous, which were paid the compliment of burning, and for which his mistress received fifty louis.

The history of the inspiration of masterpieces would afford a peculiarly interesting insight into human nature. It may be set down to the credit of Madame Puisieux (history knows of nothing else to her credit) that her rapacity at least forced this incorrigible ne'er-do-well upon his destiny, and first turned Diderot, the most delightful scamp in the capital, into Diderot the hard-working philosopher and man of genius.

Nanette came home presently, having earned the love and admiration of the little family at Langres, and put up with Madame Puisieux as best she could. Other children were born to her, and died; only one, little Angelique, survived. Of the quantity of Diderot's love for this child there is no doubt; it is only the quality that is questionable. Self-indulgent to himself, he was weakly indulgent to her. She was apt at learning, so, when they both felt inclined, he taught her music and history. Later, when she was ill, he wrote letters about her full of ardent affection; but he left her mother to nurse her and went off gaily to amuse himself with his friends, and then took great credit for having given 'orders which marked attention and interest' in her, before he went out and dined with Grimm under the trees in the Tuileries.

Of course Angelique loved the lively good-natured father much the better of the two. Of her mother the daughter herself said afterwards, with a sad truth, that she would have had a happier life if she could have cared less for her husband. However, Denis was working now, and working meant, or should mean, ease and competence.

The 'Philosophical Thoughts' had made men turn and look at him. True, their audacious freedom was not pleasing to the government; but what did a Diderot care for that? His ideas rolled off his pen as the words rolled off his tongue. 'I do not compose, I am no author,' he wrote once. 'I read, or I converse, I ask questions, or I give answers.' The lines should be placed as a motto over each of his works. That they are literally true accounts for all his defects as a writer, and for all his charm.

In 1749 he happened to be talking about a certain famous operation for cataract, and afterwards wrote down his reflections on it. To a man born blind, atheism, said Diderot, is surely a natural religion. He sent his 'Letter on the Blind for the Use of Those Who See' to the great chief of the party of which his 'Philosophical Thoughts' had proclaimed himself a member. Voltaire replied that, for his part, if he were blind, he should have recognised a great Intelligence who provided so many substitutes for sight; and the friendship between Arouet and Denis was started with a will.

On July 24, 1749, Diderot found himself a prisoner in the fortress of Vincennes. He was not wholly surprised. No literary man was astonished at being imprisoned in those days. Diderot was perfectly aware that since the publication of the 'Philosophical Thoughts' he had been suspect of the police; he was also aware that his 'Letter on the Blind' contained a sneer on the subject of a fine lady, the *chère amie* of d'Argenson, the War Minister. For company he had 'Paradise Lost' and his own buoyant temperament. He made a pen out of a toothpick, and ink out of the slate scraped from the side of his window, mixed with wine; and with characteristic good-nature wrote down this simple recipe for writing materials on the wall of his cell for the benefit of future sufferers.

Better than all, he was the friend of Voltaire, and Voltaire's Madame du Châtelet was a near relative of the governor of Vincennes. After twenty-one days of wire-pulling, Socrates Diderot, as Madame du Châtelet called him, was removed, as the fruit of her efforts, from the fortress to the castle of Vincennes, put on parole, allowed the society of his wife and children, with pen, ink, and books to his heart's content. One day Madame Puisieux came to see him—in attire too magnificent to be entirely for the benefit of a poor dog of a prisoner like myself, thinks Denis. That night he climbed over the high wall of the *enceinte* of the castle, and finding her, as he had expected, amusing herself with another admirer at a *fête*, renounced her as easily and hotly as he had fallen in love with her. He had one far more famous visitor in Vincennes, Jean Jacques Rousseau. As they walked together in the wood of Vincennes, Denis, with his overrunning fecundity of idea, suggested to Jean Jacques, it is said, the matter for that essay, sometimes called the 'Essay against Civilisation,' which first made him famous.

When his imprisonment had lasted three months Diderot, at the angry urging of the booksellers of Paris, was released.

In 1745 one of those booksellers, Le Breton, had suggested to him 'the scheme of a book that should be all books.'

Enterprising England had been first in the field. To Francis Bacon belongs the honour of having originated the idea of an Encyclopædia. Chambers, an Englishman, first worked out that idea. It was a French translation of Chambers that Le Breton took to Diderot, and it was Diderot who breathed upon it the breath of life.

That this knavish bookseller's choice should have fallen out of all men upon him, might have inclined even so whole-hearted a sceptic as Denis himself to believe in an Intelligence behind the world. He was hungry and poor, and *must* have work that would bring him bread. There were indeed thousands of persons in that position; but out of those thousands there was only one with the hot, sanguine courage to undertake so risky a scheme, with the 'fiery patience' to work it in the face of overwhelming odds, and with the exuberant genius to make it the mighty masterpiece it became.

Diderot saw its possibilities at once. In another second, as it were, he saw all he could himself do, and all he could not do. He could write about most things. He could study the trades and industries of France, if it took him thirty years of labour, of which the mere thought would daunt most men; by giving their history he could glorify for ever those peaceful arts which make a nation truly great and happy. He could write on Gallantry, on Genius, on Libraries, on Anagrams. For his fertile spirit scarcely any subject was too great or too small. Against intolerance he could bring to bear 'the concentrated energy of a profound conviction.' Religion itself he could attack in so far as it interfered with men's liberty; and miracle he must attack, because, in the words of Voltaire, 'Men will not cease to be persecutors till they have ceased to be absurd.' If he had, just to appease the authorities, and to give the book a chance of a hearing, to truckle here and there to prejudice and superstition, well, Diderot could lie as heartily and as cheerfully as he did all things.

But the inexact schoolboy of Harcourt College was no mathematician, and knew his limitations. With the freemasonry of genius he saw in a single flashing glance that d'Alembert was the man to share with him the parentage of this wonderful child. He stormed the calm savant in his attic above the glazier's shop, overwhelmed, prayed, pressed, bewitched him, and with 'his soul in his eyes and his lips' woke in d'Alembert's quiet breast an enthusiasm which was at least some reflex of his own.

For three years the two worked night and day at the preliminaries of their scheme. In 1750 Diderot poured out, with the warmth and glow of a woman in love, the Prospectus and Plan of his work. The overwhelmingness of his enthusiasm had forced a privilege for it from the authorities. Also in 1750 appeared d'Alembert's Preface, and the first volume was launched on the world.

From this time until 1765 the history of Diderot and of the Encyclopædia is the same thing. For fifteen years he worked at it unremittingly through storm and sunshine. The idea possessed and dominated him. In a garret on the fifth floor in his lodging in the Rue Taranne, wrapped in an old dressing-gown, with wild hair, bare neck, and bent back, the message he must deliver through the Encyclopædia bubbled into his heart and went straight from his heart to his pen.

'This thing will surely produce a great revolution in the human mind,' he said of it in passionate exultation: 'We shall have served humanity.' For this Diderot, who disbelieved so loudly and truculently in God, believed hopefully in the improvement of human kind, and had for the race so vast and so generous a pity that he sacrificed to it the coarse pleasures his coarse nature loved, his time, his peace, his worldly advancement, his safety, and his friend.

In 1752 a Royal Edict of matchless imbecility suppressed the first two volumes of the book, at the same time begging its promoters to continue to bring out others! Every year a volume appeared until 1757. The success of the thing was prodigious, and with reason, for it said what, so far, men had only dared to think. It gave the history, quite innocently, of the taxes—of *gabelle*, of *taille*, of *corvée*—and they stood 'damned to everlasting fame;' it showed the infamous abuses of the game-laws; it manifested the miracles of science. As by a magnet the genius of Diderot had drawn to him, as contributors, all the genius of France; while always at his side, co-editing, restraining his imprudence, yet working as he worked himself, was d'Alembert.

And then, in 1759, came the great suspension. D'Alembert had written his famous article 'Geneva,' and that mad emotionalist, Jean Jacques Rousseau, in the most famous treachery in the history of literature, turned on the philosophic party in his Letter to d'Alembert 'On Plays.' The authorities of France united with insulted Calvinism and with Rousseau, and declared the Encyclopædia accursed and forbidden. That would have been bad enough; but there was yet one thing worse. Beaten down by storm and insult, d'Alembert fell back from the fray and left Diderot to fight the battle alone.

He started up in a second, raging and cursing, and went out with his life in his hand. Seizing his pen, he slashed, hewed, hacked, with that reckless weapon on every side. Vincennes and the Bastille loomed ominously; he was never sure one day, says his daughter, of being allowed to continue the next; but he went on. The authorities might burn, but they could not destroy; they might prohibit, but they could not daunt a

II: DIDEROT: THE TALKER

Diderot.
In 1764, despite galleys and bonfires, kings, ministers, and *lettres de cachet*, the last ten volumes were ready to appear in a single issue and to crown his life's labour, when fate struck him a last crushing blow. When the manuscript of the articles had been burnt he discovered that the false Le Breton, fearing for his own safety, had cut out all such passages as he thought might endanger it; and had thus mutilated and ruined the ten volumes past recall.
Diderot burst, literally, into tears of rage. Despair and frenzy seized him. Was this to be the end? Not while he had breath in his body! He attacked Le Breton with an unclean fury not often matched, and in 1765 the volumes appeared, as whole as his talent and energy could make them. It was Diderot who said that if he must choose between Racine, bad husband, father, and friend, but sublime poet; and Racine, good husband, father, and friend, but dull ordinary man, he would choose the first. 'Of the wicked Racine, what remains? Nothing. Of Racine, the man of genius? The work is eternal.' When one considers his Herculean labours for the Encyclopædia, one is almost tempted to judge him as he judged Racine.
All the time, too, he was busy in many other ways. There has surely never been such a good-natured man of letters. The study door in the attic was open not only to all his friends, but to all the Grub Street vagrants and parasites of Paris. Diderot purified his friend d'Holbach's German-French and profusely helped his dearest Grimm in the 'Literary Correspondence;' he corrected proofs for Helvétius, Raynal, and Galiani, gave lessons in metaphysics to a German princess, and was, for himself, not only an encyclopædist, but a novelist, an art-critic, and a playwright. He also wrote dedicatory epistles for needy musicians, 'reconciled brothers, settled lawsuits, solicited pensions.' He planned a comedy for an unsuccessful dramatic author, and, in roars of laughter, indited an advertisement of a hair-wash to oblige an illiterate hairdresser. The story has been told often, but still bears telling afresh, of the young man who came to him with a personal satire against Diderot himself. 'I thought,' says the satirist, 'you would give me a few crowns to suppress it.' 'I can do better for you than that,' says Diderot, not in the least annoyed. 'Dedicate it to the brother of the Duke of Orleans, who hates me; take it to him and he will give you assistance.' 'But I do not know the Prince.' 'Sit down, and I will write the dedication for you.' He did, and so ably,

that the satirist obtained a handsome sum.
Another day he composed for the benefit of a woman, who had been deserted by the Duc de la Vrillière, a most touching appeal to the Duke's feelings. 'While I lived in the light of your love, I did not ask your pity. But of all your passion there only remains to me your portrait—and that I must sell to-morrow for bread.' The Duke sent her fifty louis.
It is hardly necessary to say that Diderot's friends availed themselves as freely of his purse as of his brains. In return for his mighty expenditure of time, talent, and energy for the Encyclopædia he never received more than the princely sum of one hundred and thirty pounds a year. As he was the sort of person who always took a carriage if he wanted one, who had a pretty taste in miniatures and *objets d'art* which he found it positively imperative to gratify, as he loved high play and always lost—as, in brief, he could never deny himself or anybody else anything—it was physically impossible he should ever be solvent.
One graceless hanger-on turned back as he was leaving him one day. 'M. Diderot, do you know any natural history?' 'Well,' says Diderot, 'enough to tell a pigeon from a humming-bird.' 'Have you ever heard of the *Formica leo*? It is a very busy little creature; it burrows a hole in the earth like a funnel, covers the surface with a fine sand, attracts a number of stupid insects to it, takes them, sucks them dry, and says, "M. Diderot, I have the honour to wish you a very good morning."' It may be said of Diderot that he could love, but not respect; and that is the inevitable attitude one takes towards himself.
In 1755, during his work at the Encyclopædia and for those innumerable idle persons who had much better have worked for themselves, poor Nanette went on a second fatal visit to Langres and gave her husband the opportunity of falling in love with Mademoiselle Volland, and starting a memorable correspondence.
Sophie Volland was a rather elderly young lady, with spectacles, and a good deal of real cleverness and erudition. Whether Diderot, who was now a man of forty-two, was ever literally in love with her, or whether he was 'less than lover but more than friend,' remains uncertain. His letters to her are warmly interesting, frank, natural, spontaneous, with many passages of exquisite beauty and thoughtfulness. There is but one fault—that fatal fault without which Diderot would not have been Diderot at all but some loftier man—his

irrepressible indecency.

He had much to tell Mademoiselle. The words seem to trip over each other in his anxiety to show her all he had done and felt. He was now famous. The Encyclopædia had thrown open to him, cutler's son though he was, the doors of the salons; a great quarrel he had with Rousseau in 1757—the dingy details of which there is neither interest nor profit in recalling—made him the talk of the *cafés*.

But this loud, explosive Denis was scarcely a social light. He said himself that he only liked company in which he could say anything. And what Diderot meant by *anything* was considered indecorous even in that freest of all free-spoken ages. Good old Madame Geoffrin lost her patience with him, not only for his licence, but for talking so movingly about duty and neglecting all his own. She was not going to ignore his Mademoiselle Volland. She treated him 'like a beast,' he said, and advised his wife to do the same. As for Madame Necker—'qui raffole de moi,' said the complacent Denis himself—she too 'judged great men by their conduct and not by their talents,' which was very awkward indeed for a Diderot.

There was a third house where he visited much more often and got on much better; but that was not because Madame d'Épinay was its mistress, but because Grimm was its presiding genius. His friendship with the cool German had a sentimentality and a demonstrativeness which Englishmen find hard to forgive, but which were sincere enough not the less. Grimm took complete control of his impulsive, generous colleague. Because Grimm bade him, Denis began in 1759 writing his 'Salons,' or criticisms on pictures, and became 'the first critic in France who made criticism eloquent;' while, when Grimm was away, almost all the work of the 'Literary Correspondence' fell on Diderot's too good-natured shoulders. When his dearest friend was not there, Diderot's steps turned much less often towards Madame d'Épinay's house.

In 1759 he first spent an autumn at the only place at which he was perfectly at home, and where he soon became a regular visitor.

Baron d'Holbach was first of all 'an atheist, and not ashamed;' but he was also very rich, very liberal, very hospitable, with a charming country house at Grandval, near Charenton, where he entertained the free-thinkers of all nations, and where his table was equally celebrated for its cook and its conversation.

The former was so good that Denis was always over-eating himself; and the latter was, in a moral sense, so bad that he enjoyed it to the utmost.

The Grandval household was fettered by none of the tiresome rules which are apt to make visiting, when one has passed the easily adaptable season of youth, a hazardous experiment. The hostess 'fulfilled no duties and exacted none.' The visitors were as free as in their own homes. Diderot would get up at six, take a cup of tea, fling open the windows to admit the air and sunshine, and then fall to work. At two came dinner. The house was always full of people who met now for the first time. In that free style, glowing with life and colour, Diderot recorded to Mademoiselle Volland the Rabelaisian conversation which made these dinners so long, and, to him, so delightful. He reported to her verbatim the amazing liberty of speech which distinguished them, just as he reported to her in minutest detail the indigestions for which the too excellent cook was responsible.

The unbridled talk of d'Holbach's mother-in-law continually set the table in a roar. Diderot himself was at his best—full of *bonhomie* and *joie-de-vivre*—laughing one minute and crying the next, warm in generous pity for sorrow, quick to be irritated or appeased, pouring out torrents of splendid ideas and then of grossest ribaldry, his mouth speaking always from the fullness of his heart, utterly indiscreet, brilliant, ingenuous, delightful; an orator 'drunk with the exuberance of his own verbosity,' who could argue that black was white, and then that white was black again, and whose seduction and danger lay in the fact that he always fully believed both impossibilities himself. No subject that was started found him cool or neutral. 'He is too hot an oven,' said Voltaire; 'everything gets burnt in him.'

When the dinner was over he would thrust his arm through his host's and walk in the garden with him. He at least did his best to imbue the dogmatic atheism of d'Holbach with luxuriance and warmth. At seven they came back to the house, and supper was followed by picquet and by talk till they went to bed.

Among many other visitors whom Diderot met while he was what he called 'veuf' at Grandval were at least four Englishmen—Sterne, Wilkes, Garrick, and Hume.

Diderot has been well called the most English of the Frenchmen of the eighteenth century. He began his literary career by making translations from our language. In a passion of admiration he had fallen at the feet of the 'divine Richardson,' and imitated 'Pamela' in a very bad novel of his own, 'The Nun;' in another, 'Jacques, the Fatalist,' he tried to accustom France to romance in the style of Sterne. He had taught his fellow-citizens, he said, to read and to esteem Bacon. He was familiar with the works of Pope, Chaucer, Tillotson, and Locke; and he has left a noble and famous criticism upon Shakespeare: 'He is like the St. Christopher of Notre-Dame, an unshapen Colossus, rudely carven, but beneath whose legs we can all walk without our brows touching him.'

To Garrick, Diderot paid exaggerated homage, and went into raptures over the wonderful play of his face. He admired Wilkes's morals as well as his mind, and in 1768 wrote him a flattering letter. As for Hume, he liked the delightful Diderot better than any other philosopher he met in France. It is Diderot who tells the story of Hume saying at d'Holbach's table, 'I do not believe there is such a thing as an atheist; I have never seen one,' and of d'Holbach's replying, 'Then you have been a little unfortunate; you are sitting now with seventeen.' Sterne, whose 'Tristram Shandy' was delighting France in general and Diderot in particular when its author was at Grandval, on his return home sent Denis English books.

In 1761 Diderot produced a play. 'The Father of the Family' is, it must be confessed, a sad bore with his lachrymose moralities; but he is exhilarating compared to 'The Natural Son,' Diderot's second play, which was acted in 1771. The universal Denis was no playwright.

In 1772 he published the ten volumes of plates which he had laboriously prepared to supplement the text of the Encyclopædia; and in May 1773, when he was sixty years old, he visited Catherine the Great.

He had had relations with her for some years. One fine day, in 1765, it had suddenly occurred to him that his dearest Angelique, over whom he had poured such streams of paternal sentiment, would have positively no *dot*. Her fond, improvident father had, of course, never attempted to save anything for her, and, if he knew his own disposition, must have known too he never would save anything. The only thing he had of value in the world, besides his head, was his library. Catherine the Great was a magnificent patron of letters; and Diderot was her especial *protégé*. He would sell his books to her! She delightedly accepted the offer. She gave him for them

a sum equal to about seven hundred pounds, and appointed him her librarian at a salary of a thousand livres a year, fifty years' payment being made in advance.
For the first time in his history Diderot found himself rich. When a patron so munificent asked him to visit her, how could he decline? All the Encyclopædists were her warm admirers; she herself used to say modestly that Voltaire had made her the fashion. Denis hated long journeys and loved Paris, but go he must. He left France on May 10, 1773. He stopped at The Hague— where he characteristically admired the beauty of the women, and the turbot—and at last arrived at St. Petersburg.
For a monarch who complained that she might have been the head of Medusa—everyone turned to stone when she entered the room—Diderot must have been a singularly refreshing guest. It was one of the most charming traits in his character that he respected persons no more than a child does, or a dog. All etiquette fled before his breezy, impulsive personality. The very clothes he arrived in were so shabby, her Majesty had to present him immediately with a court suit. He was with her every afternoon. He said what he liked, and as much as he liked, which was a very great deal. In the heat and excitement of his arguments he would hammer the Imperial knees black and blue, till the Empress had to put a table in front of her for safety. If he ever did recollect her august position, '*Allons!*' she would cry; 'between men everything is permissible.' He evolved the most magnificent, impossible schemes for the government of her empire—which would have upset it in a week if she had tried them, said she. During his stay, his dearest Grimm was also a guest. In March 1774, Denis left; and by the time he reached Paris again, was persuaded that he had enjoyed himself very much indeed.
Four years later, in 1778, he first saw in the flesh the great elder brother of his order, the master-worker in the temple slowly lifting its gorgeous towers towards the light—Voltaire. They had not always agreed on paper: their goal had been the same, but not the road to it. 'But we are not so far apart,' says old Voltaire; 'we only want a conversation to understand each other.' Accordingly, when he came on his last triumph to the capital, Diderot went to see him in the Villettes' house on what is now the Quai Voltaire. Few details of their interviews have been preserved; but it is said that they discussed Shakespeare, and that when Diderot left, Voltaire said of him: 'He is clever, but he lacks one very necessary talent—that of dialogue.' On

his part, Diderot compared Voltaire to a haunted castle falling into ruins—'but one can easily see it is still inhabited by a magician.'
Voltaire died. Diderot was himself growinh old; he had acquired, he thought in Russia, the seeds of a lung disease. Angelique married a M. de Vandeul, on the strength of the *dot* provided by the sale of the library. Madame Diderot, poor soul, had become not a little worried and embittered. It is the careless who make the careworn, and Diderot was almost to the last the engaging, light-hearted scamp whose troubles are always flung on to some patient scapegoat.
In 1783, or 1784, the death of Mademoiselle Volland gave him a real grief. Twenty years before he had written to her with an exquisite eloquence of the calm and gentle approach of the great rest, Death: 'One longs for the end of life as, after hard toil, one longs for the end of the day.' He proved in himself the truth of his own words. He had not even a hope of the immortality of the soul; but he had worked hard, the evening was come, and he was weary. He was still working—writing the 'Life of Seneca.' He was still his all too lovable, spontaneous self, talking with that marvellous inspiration of which the best of his books can convey little idea.
A fortnight before he died he moved into a new home, given him by Catherine the Great, in the Rue Richelieu, opposite the birthplace of Molière and almost next door to the house where Voltaire had lived with Madame du Châtelet, and after her death. The *curé* of Saint-Sulpice came to see him, and suggested that a retractation of his sceptical opinions would produce good effect. 'I dare say it would,' said Denis, 'but it would be a most impudent lie.' In his last conversation Madame de Vandeul records that she heard him say: 'The first step towards philosophy is unbelief.'
The end came very suddenly. On the last day of July 1784, he was supping with his wife and daughter, and at dessert took an apricot. Nanette gently remonstrated. 'Mais que diable de mal veux-tu que cela me fasse?' he cried. They were his last words and perfectly characteristic. He died as he sat, a few minutes later.
If to be great means to be good, then Denis Diderot was a little man. But if to be great means to do great things in the teeth of great obstacles, then none can refuse him a place in the temple of the Immortals.
His fiction, taken from rottenness, has returned to it, and is justly dead. His plays were damned on their appearance. His

moving criticisms on art and the drama, his satirical dialogue, 'Rameau's Nephew'—nearly all the printed talk of this most matchless of all talkers—are rarely read. His letters to Mademoiselle Volland will last so long as the proper study of mankind is man. But it is as the father of the Encyclopædia that Denis Diderot merits eternal recognition. Guilty as he was in almost every relation of life towards the individual, for mankind, in the teeth of danger and of infidelity, at the ill-paid sacrifice of the best years of his exuberant life, he produced that book which first levelled a free path to knowledge and enfranchised the soul of his generation.

III: GALIANI: THE WIT

'How can you say I do not know Galiani?' wrote Voltaire to Madame d'Épinay. 'I have read him; therefore I have seen him.'
Of that Brotherhood of Progress, united by a love, sometimes for each other and always for mankind, if Voltaire was the leader, and d'Alembert the thinker, Galiani was certainly the wit. In his own day he was celebrated as the man who made Paris laugh—and ponder—by his famous 'Dialogues on Corn;' and in our day he is remembered as the gay little buffoon of the eighteenth century and the author of a most amusing correspondence. Voltaire went on to declare the Abbé must be as much like his Dialogues as two jets of fire are like each other; and Diderot swore that if he had written a word of the book, he *must* have written it exactly as it was.
Light, sparkling, irresponsible, like the brillleast hampered by respect for the *convenances*, as quick and flashing as sunshine on diamonds, as bubbling and spontaneous as a dancing little mountain torrent, perfectly free from the bitterness, the malignity, and the sarcasm which make Voltaire's jests so terrible—the talk and the writing of Galiani are alike unique. The 'dear little Abbé' of the women, with his dwarf's figure and his great head, his crafty Italian brain to conceive a brilliant scheme and his easy flow of wit to present it to his world, stands out alone against the horizon of the eighteenth century.
Ferdinand Galiani first saw the light at Chieti, in Abruzzo, on December 2, 1728. He was born with a silver spoon in his mouth, in two senses at least. His father was Royal Auditor in one of the provinces of the Neapolitan Government; and his uncle was Monseigneur Celestin Galiani, first chaplain to the King of Naples, and a most wealthy, learned, and enlightened churchman.
Little Ferdinand was eight when he was sent to be educated, with his elder brother, Bernard, under this uncle's supervision at Naples. For a time the two children were taught at the convent of the Celestins, as Monseigneur was in Rome, negotiating a peace on behalf of the King of the Two Sicilies. When he returned, he took the boys back to his own palace and gave them the best and the most delightful of all forms of learning, the society of clever people. The visitors soon recognised that the way to the uncle's heart was through the

precocious brain of the little nephew—that to teach Ferdinand was to delight Monseigneur. Whatever brother Bernard may have been, Ferdinand was surely the aptest and sharpest of infant prodigies. He heard discussed around him antiquarianism, history, literature, commerce; and not one seed of information fell on barren ground. Many years after Grimm declared that there was only one man in Paris who really knew Latin, and he was the Abbé Galiani.

He was still a mere boy when he represented Bernard at a meeting of the Academy of Naples and read an article on the Immaculate Conception. The worthy Academicians, naturally shocked at such a little creature attempting a subject so serious, forbade him to read it. 'Very well,' thinks young Ferdinand, 'I can wait.' The executioner of Naples died soon after. The Academy was famous for its *éloges funèbres*. And behold, there appears, in wicked and most unmistakable travesty of the Academical funeral orations, the *éloge* of the executioner! The Academy was very indignant, the world very much amused, and Galiani had made his bow to the public in the *rôle* he was never to relinquish. He confessed all to the First Minister, Tanucci. Tanucci introduced him to the King and Queen of Naples, who were delighted, and then appeased the Academy by condemning the delinquent to ten days' spiritual exercises in a neighbouring convent.

At sixteen the boy was already an ardent Political Economist. As England was the country where that science was brought to perfection, he learnt English, translated Locke's 'Essay on Money,' and set to work to write one himself. All the time he was studying diligently the ancient navigation, peoples, and commerce of the Mediterranean, throwing off a satire here, a mocking set of verses there, and cultivating that pretty talent for epigram and story-telling.

When 'Money' was finished, he read it to Monseigneur, without mentioning its authorship. 'Why do not *you* give your mind to serious works such as that?' said the King's chaplain, and praised the thing extravagantly. When Galiani told his secret, Monseigneur was so delighted that he at once set to work at Court to procure this promising nephew something really worth having. At two-and-twenty years old, having never studied theology and having taken minor orders only, and with the sole object of obtaining these emoluments, Galiani found himself the possessor of the benefice of Centola and the abbey of Saint-Laurent, while a dispensation from Rome gave him the title of Monseigneur and the honour of the mitre. Soon after, the admiring Court of Naples also presented him with the rich abbey of Saint Catherine of Celano.

The wonder is, not that Galiani writhed with laughter (like the little Punchinello his friends dubbed him) when he alluded to the religion of his fathers, but that to the end of his days he saw in that religion, beneath its shameless venality and its hideous moral corruptions, some saving truth to bless and comfort man's soul. When all Paris laughed at the credulity of Madame Geoffrin, whose death was said to have been brought about from over-devotion to her religious duties, it was Galiani who wrote that he considered that unbelief was 'the greatest effort the mind of man could make against his natural instincts and wishes. ... As the soul grows old, belief reappears.' Unlike nearly all his philosophic friends, if his own illusions were few, he was careful to leave undisturbed those of happier people.

In respect to the emoluments he received from Rome, and on which he fattened all his life, it may be justly said that he took them as a man takes a fortune out of a business he knows to be rotten, congratulating himself on his own perspicacity, and believing that beneath the rottenness there still lies the making of a true and honest enterprise.

The Neapolitan Government having adopted all the ideas suggested in 'Money,' the fortunate young gentleman who had written it started off in excellent spirits, in November 1751, for Rome, Florence, and Venice. The Pope, and all the grandees, *savants*, and *littérateurs* in Italy petted and made much of the agreeable little prodigy.

In June 1753 his uncle, Celestin, died, leaving Ferdinand his fortune. Galiani still remained in Naples, the spirit and the delight of the brilliant society that Monseigneur had gathered about him. But there was never any time in his life when it was enough for this wit to be wit only. He said of himself that he had all the vices, and his friends declared he had all the tastes. The friends were right. He soon began to make a collection of the stones thrown up by Vesuvius, classified them, wrote a beautiful dissertation on them, and sent them to the Pope with the inscription, *Holy Father, command that these stones be made bread*. Benedict the Fourteenth was a comfortable person who loved a joke and thought it worth its reward. He replied by giving the little Abbé yet another benefice, Amalfi, worth three hundred ducats. Then, of course, the Geological Academy of Herculaneum must do something more for such a lively geologist than merely make him a

member of its body: it presented him with a pension.
In 1758 this spoilt child of fortune had the honour of composing Pope Benedict's funeral oration. Then he was made Chancellor to the King, and, in 1759, Secretary to the Embassy in Paris.
It was the turning-point of his life, and the greatest event of his history. But for that appointment, he might have been nothing, after all, but some brilliant little local light, with his sparkling Southern talents only employed for the advantage of Italy and certainly never heard of beyond her borders. To it he owed all his fame and the gayest and most successful epoch in his existence. To it the world owes its picture of the man himself, the 'Dialogues on Corn,' and the Correspondence with Madame d'Épinay.
Galiani was at first pleased to go. But he was thirty years old, and had never yet been out of his own country. She had done generously by him, and he was extremely rich. On the other hand, the secretaryship involved further large emoluments, and Galiani was not one of those rare, wise people who know how easy it is to be rich enough; he had not learned from the possession of money how very little it can buy. Paris was then not only the capital of France, but the social capital of the world. She was at the height of her ancient glory. Revolutions had not shattered her splendid buildings or the delicate fabric of the most easy, polished, accomplished society under heaven. She was the finishing school of Europe. Her language was the language of many Courts, of Frederick of Prussia, and of the letters of Catherine the Great. From her printing presses she poured forth, almost daily, masterpieces of literature, or pamphlets which were to change dynasties and shake kingdoms. On her throne sat Louis the Fifteenth, as rotten as the society of which he was the head, but, like that society, with a rottenness covered by a magnificence which awed investigation into silence. Choiseul was the minister in name, and Madame de Pompadour in reality; and over the *salons*, then in the height of their power and distinction, presided women 'who in the decline of their beauty revealed the dawn of their intelligence.'
Such a world should have pleased Galiani, or any happy Southerner who loved to bask in the warmth of prosperity and shrug his shoulders at the possibility of future disaster. But at first it did not. He was cold and homesick. His health, he wrote, would certainly not survive the unequal climate. Foreign customs, bad air, detestable water, everything here is

noxious to my Italian temperament! Then Choiseul received the petted wit of the Neapolitan parties coldly, nonchalantly, indifferently. And Versailles—Versailles was yet more objectionable. When Galiani was presented there in June 1760, with his four-and-a-half-foot figure overladen with the ridiculous gala dress of the period, the men burst into open laughter and the women sneered behind their fans. Why should that cruel age, which had no compassion on the helplessness of little children, on poverty, on misfortune, on weakness, and which, when it did not mock at moral suffering, fled from it as from a disease one might catch—why should such an age pity the sensibilities of a deformed little foreigner, an absurd dwarf of an abbé, whom no one in Paris (which is to say the world) had ever heard of before? Galiani was more than a match for the laughers. 'Sire,' he said to the King, 'you now see only a sample of the secretary; the secretary will arrive later.' The King was delighted; but the secretary retired with that cruel laughter ringing in his heart. For a whole year he pleaded passionately for his recall. He wrote bitterly of the French as 'a mobile and superficial race full at once of passion and lightness. ... My clothes, my character, my way of thinking, and all my natural defects will always make me insupportable to this people and to myself.' From being the most popular and successful man in Naples, he was in Paris the insignificant secretary at whom, as he passed by, men mocked with the tongue in the cheek. They did not indeed mock for ever. His own sharp tongue was bound to win him respect and reputation. First it was a jest uttered here; and then a story, with his own inimitable gesticulation, told there. This little secretary is going to be amusing! Further, he was always accompanied by his *âme damnée*, the most intelligent of monkeys, who was only something less entertaining than his master. The master, moreover, could play on the clavecin, and sing to it, wonderfully. Even for the Parisians of that day his conversation was free, naïf, unhampered. The man has ideas, as we all have, on the liberty of the Press and the Masses, on the Deluge that is coming after us; only he can put those ideas so that the expression reads like a romance or sounds like a jest!
Then he was introduced to Baron Gleichen, and to Grimm, the first journalist in Europe. Grimm made him known to Madame d'Épinay; and his acquaintance with her, with Madame Necker, with Madame Geoffrin, and with

Mademoiselle de Lespinasse, implied an introduction to the society of all witty Paris, and of all travelling England. He became the friend of d'Alembert, who had just published his 'Elements of Philosophy,' of Diderot, of d'Holbach, of Helvétius, of Morellet, and of Marmontel. He met that magnificent icicle, Saint Lambert, still writing his 'Seasons' and stealing Madame d'Houdetot from Rousseau. He knew Suard, Thomas, Raynal, and that picturesque and ill-fated young Spaniard, the Marquis de Mora.

In a word, by 1760, Galiani was launched—the gayest little skiff that ever danced into a summer sea. The Parisian climate improved in the twinkling of an eye; the bad water became drinkable; the light and fickle people turned into one 'loving and worthy to be loved.' Some fool of a wit, who had declared that the Abbé would never succeed at Court because he thought too loud and spoke too low, must needs eat his words. However low he spoke now, the audience always heard. They expected a *bon mot* or a *naïveté*, every time he opened his mouth, and he did not disappoint them. Instead of a poor little dwarf from that God-forsaken Naples, the secretary became 'the prettiest little Harlequin Italy has produced,' 'the incomparable Abbé,' 'the head of Machiavelli,' 'Machiavellino,' 'ce drôle de Napolitain,' 'Plato, with the verve and gestures of Harlequin.' In a word, he was the mode. The women raved about him—he understood them so well!—and fought among each other for his presence at their parties. If Choiseul remained cold, his Duchess—'the gentlest, amiablest, civil little creature that ever came out of a fairy egg,' said Horace Walpole—was as fond of her Abbé as were her society sisters. Galiani was asked everywhere and went everywhere. He had found his true element at last. How tame and provincial the Neapolitan parties looked now! How dull and restricted were ambitions that limited one to Italy! Paris was the theatre of Europe—with a crowded audience of all nations watching, half laughing and half afraid, the next move in her breathless tragi-comedy. There was hardly ever a more effective actor on her boards than this buffoon, this keen-set little wit, this jester, with here and there, now and then, as if by accident, some poignant meaning, some thrilling prophecy beating beneath his jests, and startling his hearers to a brief and sudden gravity.

In spite of the facts that Galiani was busy learning French, making a Commentary on Horace, and working at the duties of his secretaryship with an entirely superfluous energy, his

III: GALIANI: THE WIT

social life in Paris began early in the morning. It was his custom to stop in bed till the middle of the day and thus receive his friends; *tenir son lit de justice,* he called it. Sometimes he would wrap himself up, and sit on the bed with his little legs crossed like a tailor. He talked a great deal—a great deal too much, said some people; he had no 'flashes of silence.' When his friend began speaking he waited impatiently to leap into the conversation himself; and when the friend attempted to make himself heard, 'Let me finish,' says the Abbé,' you will have plenty of time to answer me back;' but he took good care that that time never came. 'Paris,' he used to say regretfully in later years, 'is the only place where they listened to me;' and one of his biographers declares pathetically that he died of 'paroles rentrées et non écoutées.'

No wonder he was so full of life in the French capital. The talk of the morning was always followed by more talk in the evening. On Thursdays, it was Madame Geoffrin's turn to receive. This 'nurse of philosophy,' this calm, placid, old hostess with her quiet, orthodox principles, and her prudent, regular life, could no more help loving this little libertine of a wit than could her lighter sisters. He was 'her abbé, her little abbé, her *petite chose.*' As for him, he loved her without afterthought, and with the whole-hearted impetuosity of his nature. He declared that she inspired him with wit, that her arm-chairs were the tripods of Apollo and he was the Sibyl. Her very primness egged him on to more reckless stories, to wilder buffooneries; but he went away laughing at her and loving her and respecting her, and did all to the end of his life. There was another woman whom he also respected, but whom he did not love. With her one intense, overmastering passion centred on her husband, Madame Necker was for ever the Calvinist pastor's daughter, 'rigid, frigid, and good.' One female friend spoke of her acrimoniously as 'soaked in starch,' and Galiani himself complained, without by any means intending a compliment, of her 'cold demeanour of decency.' How such a ribald, rollicking person as himself ever gained admittance to a Puritan household would be a wonder in our day; but in that day if, as Galiani himself wrote, one was only to know virtuous people, the number of one's friends would be alarmingly reduced. And—and—Madame Necker's salon was not for herself or her acquaintance; it was for her husband. Across the dinner-table on those Fridays the lively and daring Italian would defend with his rapid, reckless tongue the causes which his heavy host could only maintain with his pen. Leaning after dinner against the chimney corner, with his sparkling eyes lighting up his keen pale face, with his dwarfs figure dressed always with an infinite neatness and nicety, Galiani would fight single-handed that battle against the Economists, his own and Necker's special antipathies, and fight it, too, against such men as Thomas, Raynal, and Morellet. No wonder Madame Necker overlooked her visitor's peccadilloes. The little Abbé had such a resistless torrent of logic! If the other side had reason in its favour, no one had a chance of advancing that reason. Directly anyone else began to talk, Galiani slipped away, and, there being no Opposition, Parliament rose.

After the orthodoxy of Madame Geoffrin and the decency of Madame Necker, the gatherings of Baron d'Holbach at Grandval might have been supposed to have afforded Galiani an agreeable contrast. Not content with disbelieving himself, the Baron's scepticism was of that eager and proselytising kind which must for ever be destroying the faith of others. He delivered himself of it with a daring irreverence that made even the Italian Abbé shudder, though, heaven knows! he talked freely enough himself, and had listened to free enough talk from others. He was here, as he had been at the Neckers', almost alone in the Opposition. It delighted him to lean over the table and assure these persons who were for pushing throne and Church, King and priest, down the abyss as fast as might be, that he loved despotism, 'bien cru, bien vert, bien âpre.' It was Galiani who alone perceived that these wild theories, conceived in *salons*, must, when translated into deeds, first of all destroy those who conceived them, and that a change in the Constitution, which might be a very beautiful thing when done, was a very vile thing in the doing. 'It worries two or three generations,' he said, 'and only obliges posterity. Posterity is merely a possibility, and we are realities. And why should realities put themselves out for possibilities?' One day at d'Holbach's, the conversation on the Deity became so outrageous, that, with every man's hand against him, Galiani rose. '*Messieurs les Philosophes*,' says he, 'you go too fast. If I were the Pope, I should hand you over to the Inquisition; if the King, to the Bastille. But as I have the good luck to be neither, I shall come to dinner next Thursday, and you shall listen to me as patiently as I have listened to you.' Thursday came. After dinner and coffee, the Abbé takes an armchair, crosses his legs, removes his wig (the night being sultry), and, with those lively gesticulations which he can no more help than he can help breathing, tells a story.

'Please suppose, gentlemen, that one of you, who is the most convinced that this world is the result of chance, happens to be playing at dice, not in a gambling hell but in one of the best houses in Paris. His adversary, casting one, two, three, four—many times—always throws number six. After the game has gone on a little while, my friend Diderot, we will say, who is losing his money, will certainty call out, "The dice are cogged! This is some swindlers' den!" What, philosopher, what? Because ten or twelve throws of dice come out of the box so that you lose half a dozen francs, you are firmly convinced that this is the result of a clever design, an artificial combination, a complicated roguery; and yet, seeing in the universe a mighty number of combinations a thousand times more difficult, more complicated, and more useful, you do not suspect that Nature's dice are also cogged, and that above there is a great Arranger?'

It was a most happy illustration, if not a convincing argument. But the age which was swayed by the eloquence of Rousseau always preferred an example to a reason: while the class who laughed later at 'The Marriage of Figaro' might certainly be counted on to enjoy a joke against itself.

There was a fourth *salon* where Galiani was much more at home than at Grandval, or under the prim wings of Madame Necker or the motherly feathers of Madame Geoffrin. At Madame d'Épinay's alone, he was perfectly natural, his rollicking, buffooning, all-daring self, able, as only a Southerner is able, to make himself entirely ridiculous without being at all contemptible.

Madame d'Épinay was that clever wife of a ruined Farmer General, who had been petted by Rousseau, and played with by Voltaire. Madame d'Houdetot was her sister-in-law; Diderot was her constant associate; Grimm was her lover; and Galiani became, and remained for twenty years, her most sincere and admiring friend.

A Platonic friendship is perhaps only possible when one or other of the Platonists is in love with a third person. Grimm, with his well-regulated head and heart, was not only perfectly able to keep a fickle woman true to him, but himself to retain an honest regard for the Abbé and to use his opinions and his wit for the 'Literary Correspondence.'

Madame d'Épinay's *salon* was of all *salons* the most thoroughly characteristic of the time and the people. No one had any duty but to amuse himself. From early in the morning, a few charming and accomplished women, who always relegated their children to servants, their stupid husbands to oblivion, and their households to chance, talked delightfully over their embroidery (with which the fashion demanded they should toy) to men, of whom among many astounding characteristics, not the least astounding is their prodigious idleness coupled with their prodigious literary production.

Galiani himself was the greatest attraction Madame d'Épinay's circle could claim. When he came in on a dripping country afternoon at La Chevrette, or in some murky winter twilight in Paris, there came with him, said Diderot, light, brightness, gaiety, folly, mirth—everything which makes one forget the cares of life. Mademoiselle d'Ette, who was at once her hostess's worst and dearest friend, looked up from her embroidery frame with her stealthy eyes aglow to welcome an acquisition so delightful. Madame d'Épinay was, as ever, gay, caressing, *insouciante*. Diderot was in ecstasies (he was always in an ecstasy about something) at the little Italian's arrival. He was a perfect treasure on a wet day! If the toy-shops made Galianis, everybody would buy one!

The Abbé takes his seat, cross-legged as usual, and from that head which was 'a library of anecdotes,' reels out a dozen stories, acting them all with an inimitable liveliness, while his hearers laugh till they cry.

A few of those stories sound dull in print, or have lost point with their youth; many more disgust modern taste by their elegant indecency. But the man who dubbed Paris, 'the *Café de l'Europe*,' d'Holbach, 'the *maître d'hotel* of philosophy,' and the vaunted liberty of the Apostles of the Social Contract, 'the right of interfering in other people's business,' still proves his title of wit. It was Galiani too who defined the death of Maria Theresa as 'an ink-bottle spilt over the map of Europe;' and Sophie Arnould's exquisite lost voice as 'the most beautiful asthma' he ever heard. It was Galiani who said that suffering was the cart-horse, and *ennui* the horse in the rich man's stable. It was Galiani who declared that the Jesuits lengthened the Creed and shortened the Decalogue that they might succeed better in the world, and Galiani who affirmed that the priests had changed the name of the Sacrament from *Pénitence* to Confession, because they thought it sufficient to avow their sins without correcting them. Finally, it was Galiani who proved that he knew intimately one side of the life around him, when he declared that the women of the eighteenth century loved with their minds, not with their hearts. Always inimitably good-humoured, never bored, never weary, ready to play on the clavecin or sing in the most charming voice in the world if the audience should tire of his conversation, seeing the ridiculous side of any subject in a flash, prompt with an anecdote to fit the most unforeseen occasion—'the little creature born at the foot of Vesuvius,' clown, harlequin, Punchinello—whatever men called him— was, and is, without counterpart in social history. There will be and have been—there certainly were in the eighteenth century—many agreeable young gentlemen who not only often dined out, but who entirely lived and fattened on a pretty taste in stories and *bons mots*, and a constant readiness to make fools of themselves for the benefit of an idle audience afraid of being bored; but there was rarely, if ever, a buffoon of such vast and solid erudition, of mental capacities so great and so varied, and of mental achievements so momentous, as the Abbé Galiani.

While the *salons* were petting and spoiling him, while he seemed to be doing nothing but talk from morning till night and from night until morning, while he was regarded as such a complete and irresistible joke that people laughed at his very name, he had yet worked so hard as Secretary to the Embassy and Charge d'Affaires that he raised the whole diplomatic corps to a worthier position, and advanced the interests of Naples with a steadiness and persistency usually allotted to a very different character. His Majesty Louis the Fifteenth presented him with a box set in diamonds. Choiseul's light indifference changed into a cool consideration. All the time the man was writing, observing, thinking. Was he a politician *pour rire*? He seemed to be everything *pour rire*. But after all, who knows? The men who had laughed the most heartily at his absurdities, turned and looked at him again with a wonder in their eyes.

In 1765 he obtained a year's leave of absence and went home to take the baths of Ischia. In 1766, on the invitation of the Marquis Caraccioli, Italian Ambassador, he went to stay in London.

It must be recorded regretfully that the Abbé did not find Britain or the British at all to his taste. David Hume said indignantly that though he only remained two months in our country, talked himself the whole time, and would not allow an Englishman to put in a word, yet when he came away he dogmatised on the character of the nation all the rest of his life as if he had never studied anything else. That he did not share the Anglomania of Voltaire is certainly true. Some years later, to one of his correspondents, he defined the English rather happily as 'the best educated nation in the world, and consequently the greatest, the most troublesome, and the most melancholy.' But some at least of his letters abuse England very freely. It was, no doubt, as difficult for the Britons to understand a Galiani as for a Galiani to understand them; and not at all wonderful that he carried away from our shores an impression of an Englishman as a solid, emotionless person, who resented buffoonery as an insult, never uttered a joke or saw one, and had all the qualities which make a nation mighty and an individual disagreeable.

The Abbé was a somewhat graver man himself when he came back to Paris. He was now thirty-eight years old, a little less free of tongue, a thought less sceptical in religion. His letters of the time contain grave observations on the Seven Years' War, and on the condition of the Paris Parliament. But he was still about the *salons*, still Parisian to the finger-tips, and he still loved Paris from his soul.

And in 1769, like a clap of thunder, came the *foudroyant* news of his recall to Naples.

Recalled! The hostesses of Paris looked at each other in dismay. Recalled! It is surely the end of all things if some political exigency, some party question, is allowed to interfere with our amusements like this! Is it Choiseul, who has protected the Economists, while Galiani hated them, who has done this thing? The exact reason for it was then matter of speculation, and is so still. It was enough, more than enough, that it was a fact that this dear, merry, little Abbé must pack up his trunks and go out of light into darkness, out of the sunshine of social favour in which he had basked and purred and gambolled, into the gloom of the provincial obscurity from which he had come.

If Paris was struck with dismay, Galiani himself was overwhelmed by the greatest calamity of his life. He declared that he had never wept at anything, not even the death of his relations, so much as at leaving Paris. 'They have torn me from Paris,' he cried, 'and they have torn out my heart.' He swore that the only good thing that wearisome Mr. Sterne, the English author, 'ever uttered was when he said to me, "It is better to die in Paris than to live in Naples."' He wrung his hands, and bemoaned out loud, according to his temperament. He followed his departure by letters to Madame d'Épinay and to d'Alembert which are really pathetic. He was also leaving behind him in Paris a woman to whom he was tied by an attachment, not Platonic. He was torn, in brief, from everything—friends and mistress, career, work, play—life itself. No wonder despair seized his soul. He went, and in parting flung into the camp of the Economists, whom he believed to be the enemy responsible for his overthrow, a bomb whose explosion rang through Europe.

In 1770 there appeared in Paris the 'Dialogues on the Corn Trade.' The taxation of, or free trade in, grain had long been a vexed question, not only in the minds of politicians but in the minds of all intelligent Frenchmen. Free Food! cried the Economist, rich in the support of Turgot and of Choiseul. Tax it! replied their opponents, mighty with the strength of Terrai, the graceless Controller-General, and the growing influence of Necker.

Through the wit and the parties, in the midst of ardent secretarial duties and of continual literary studies, somehow, at some time—though how and at what time it would be difficult to say—Galiani had brought to bear on the question his Italian shrewdness and brilliancy, all the learning and observation taught him by his uncle, and the judgment and the wisdom taught him by Heaven. No man would have believed that such a merry, light, social person could have pondered so deeply; no one *had* believed it. The book was in the form of a dialogue between a Marquis and a Chevalier. It was as gay and rollicking as the little Abbé's own talk. In fact, it was his own talk; but it was something much more. It was much more even than a pamphlet on a passing question, on a matter of local momentary importance. 'Read between the lines and in the margin,' it was an able work on the science of government, what Grimm called justly 'the production of a sound and enlightened philosopher, and of a statesman.' In it the author exposed his theory that a man of State must know not only his business but the human heart—'You must study men before you can rule them.' This knowledge he denied to Turgot; and he warned France, in solemn prophecy to be fulfilled too soon, to beware in her rulers, not the rogues and the knaves—they soon show themselves in their true colours —but *l'honnête homme trompé*. 'He wishes all men well, so all men trust him; but he is deceived as to the means of doing well.'

The work was received with the wildest enthusiasm. In far

Ferney, the spirited old Patriarch of Literature jumped for joy, almost literally, at a wit and a style so inimitable. No man ever reasoned so agreeably before… 'No man has ever made famine so amusing. … If the work does not diminish the price of bread, it will give pleasure to the whole nation. … Plato and Molière have combined to write it…' Excellent! excellent! And in the same year, 1770, the master himself wrote for his 'Questions on the Encyclopædia' the article on Grain wherein Galiani was not forgotten.

Diderot, who, with Grimm and Madame d'Épinay, had helped to correct the proofs of the 'Dialogues,' declared impetuously to Mademoiselle Volland that he had gone down on his knees to implore Galiani to publish them. Grimm said that if he were Controller-General he should attach the Abbé to France, if it cost the King forty thousand livres per annum, 'without any other stipulation but that he should amuse himself and come twice a week to chat with me over the affairs of my Government.' Even Fréron, Élie Fréron, the brilliant Parisian journalist, who hated Voltaire and consequently all Voltaire's colleagues and disciples, could not help praising the thing in his 'Literary Year.' Frederick the Great wrote the author a flattering letter.

The book's foes advertised it even better than its friends. At first, the leaders in the Economist camp looked at each other in dismay. Granted that they had justice and reason on their side, what could justice and reason do in the Paris of 1770 against that bubbling, sparkling wit? The capital must, first of all, be amused. What use, then, to advance the always doubtful argument that a writer cannot be at once gay and trustworthy, that if he is really worth hearing he can never be heard without a yawn?

The Abbé Morellet, as large as Galiani was small, and as ponderous in style as the Abbé was light, was employed to answer him. The good man wrote his refutation with such haste and ardour that the skin of his little finger was completely worn off from much rubbing against the side of his desk. And, after all, no one read him. He may, or may not, be right; he is certainly dull!

Then Turgot took up a mightier pen and wielded a mightier influence. Noble and disinterested, a better and a greater man than Galiani, the Statesman of that company of which the Abbé was but the Wit, Turgot sought, as did Galiani, the good and the progress of humanity; but he sought it by a different road, and by the labour of his whole life. He recognised the cleverness of the book; a bad cause, said he, could not be maintained with more grace and cleverness. But my little brother the Abbé is wrong, not the less. In the 'Dialogues' there peeped out, thought Turgot, something of the comfortable indifference of those who are content to leave the world as it is because it goes so smoothly with them, something of the laziness and the selfishness that come naturally to a little writer himself so comfortably beneficed and mitred. Galiani lacked, in fact, Turgot's 'instincts of the heart which teach the head.'

Right or wrong—*l'honnête homme trompé* perhaps—Turgot had put his soul into the great cause of humanity, and Galiani had only put his mind. What wonder that they saw the same world with different eyes, and would have worked out the salvation of falling France, by methods not only opposite but opposed?

Galiani went back to Naples. For many months, for years, his letters are full of his book, that effort which, even if misdirected, proved that he was no drone in the hive, that he too had that one great virtue common to all the philosophers and redeeming half their sins—he had heard the trumpet-call of responsibility towards his fellows, and had answered it. After Paris, Naples was not merely dull, it was extinction. The poor little Abbé bemoaned his fate to Madame d'Épinay in the most touching of all jesting letters. True, there was society here, and Galiani was its lion. But what society! There was Lady Orford, Robert Walpole's daughter-in-law, who had a country house close to Galiani's at Santo Sorio, at the foot of Vesuvius, and there was Sir William Hamilton, now British envoy and, to be, the husband of Lady Hamilton. Presently there came, too, the Marquis of Lansdowne, who was amiable, which, said Galiani, 'is a very rare thing for an Englishman, and Secretary of State, which is a very common thing.'

But the Abbé hated the English; and he was bored to death. The Court of Naples gave him more lucrative posts—and though he described himself as *avide* without being *avare*, which meant that he was greedy of money and yet lavish in spending it—money, even when it does not beget *ennui*, certainly never destroys it. He turned to his museum full of medals and bronzes, pictures and weapons—and that bored him too. Paris, Paris! He hankered after it for ever, 'What is the good of inoculation here,' he grumbled, after expressing delight in that discovery, 'when living itself is not worth while?' 'What a life!' he wrote dismally to d'Holbach in 1770.

'Nothing amusing here … no edicts … no suspensions of payment … no quarrels about anything—not even about religion. Dear Paris, how I regret you!'

In 1771 died there that Madame Daubiniere to whom he had been attached by no Platonic tie, and whom he had not hesitated to recommend to the good offices of Madame d'Épinay; and in the same year the death of Helvétius, the rich and amiable ex-Farmer-General, 'left a blank in the line of our battalion.' 'Let us love each other the better, we who remain,' says Galiani. 'Close the lines. Advance! Fire!' He was always declaring he had no heart; but it was there, under the lava of worldliness and mockery, as Pompeii and Herculaneum lay hid beneath the lava of his own Vesuvius. He was soon busy procuring a post at Court for his unsuccessful brother Bernard—Bernard, who had a large family, little money, and the dull bookworm talents that bring no more. Then Bernard died, and up starts the Abbé in a new *rôle*. There are three stupid nieces to be married, to say nothing of the widow! The indefatigable uncle found the girls eligible husbands, although one of them, as he wrote frankly, was as ugly as a hunchback. Then he discovered some one to marry his sister-in-law. 'If this goes on,' he wrote to Madame d'Épinay, 'people will clap when I go into my box at the theatre.'

Presently the King of Naples gave him yet two more posts—entailing not only emoluments but work—and he resumed his literary labours, wrote a pamphlet on the 'Instincts and Habitual Tastes of Man,' a comic opera, to Paisiello's music, called 'The Imaginary Socrates,' and another most amusing pamphlet, written in a single night, to distract the Neapolitans from their fright on the eruption of Vesuvius in 1779.

In 1781 he visited Eome, and was courted by all the great people; and when he came home Naples gave him another rich abbey and another most lucrative civil appointment. He was still a comparatively young man. Fortune had overturned her horn at his feet. 'The torment of all things accomplished, the plague of nought to desire,' might well have been Galani's. But he had the rare power of finding happiness where it most often hides—in small and common things. The monkey which had amused his leisure he had replaced by a couple of cats, and it afforded him infinite amusement to watch their gambols and their habits, and write long dissertations on the natural history of the animal to Madame d'Épinay in Paris. His friendship with her had lasted without break or blot for nearly five-and-twenty years. If happiness meant only

exemption from suffering, then well for Galiani that no woman ever held his heart more nearly than this light, bright, irresponsible little person. But that side of existence which brings the deepest sorrow brings too the highest joy, and who is spared the first, misses the second. Madame Daubiniere had touched neither his soul nor his life; Madame d'Épinay only aroused a capacity for a friendship which, as he loved no one, had certainly assumed some of the absorption of a passion. When she died in 1783, he stood in the presence of a great and a most genuine sorrow. She had represented the Paris he would see no more; to answer her letters had been a large occupation in his life—and she was dead! He turned to his work as his last hope, to the one means that was left of making life endurable. In 1785 he was attacked by apoplexy, and two years later he travelled for his health. But it was not improved. 'The dead are so bored,' he said in his old jesting manner; 'they have asked me to come and cheer them a little.'
In the October of 1787 the King and Queen of Naples commanded him to meet them at Portici. He went, but he was long past receiving pleasure from such honours. The Sovereigns were struck with his altered appearance, and begged him to consult a doctor. Queen Caroline wrote him a letter imploring him to renounce his scepticism and make ready for heaven. He answered with dignity and respect; but no physician for either the soul or the body could aid him now. He kept his gaiety to the last. As he had loved in life to be surrounded by friends, they were about his deathbed. He declared to them that he felt no sorrow in dying, save that he would fain have lived to publish his book on Horace. The night before his death Gatti, his friend and doctor, told him he had refused an invitation to the opera from the Ambassador of France to be near his friend. 'Ah,' says Galiani, 'you still look on me as Harlequin? Well, perhaps I shall prove more amusing than the opera.' And he did. Two hours before his death General Acton, the Prime Minister, called to see him. 'Tell his Excellency I cannot receive him. My carriage is at the door. Warn him to prepare his own.'
He died on October 30, 1787, aged nearly fifty-nine.
Dagonet, King's Fool at Arthur's Court, could not avert his master's ruin, but, noblest of all Fools, he tried. Galiani, with his laughing bells jingling in those 'Dialogues,' spoke his message in jests and could not help starving France, nor even postpone by an hour the raid on the bakers' shops in the Faubourg St. Antoine. But he, too, did his best.

IV: VAUVENARGUES: THE APHORIST

The proverb is indigenous to Spain, verse to Italy, and the aphorism to France. In that form of speech in which, in Vauvenargues' own words. La Rochefoucauld had 'turned men from virtue by persuading them that it is never genuine,' Vauvenargues vindicated human goodness, showed man that the best way to reform the world is to reform himself, and taught him how to use the freedom Voltaire gave him.
In his delicate thoughtfulness, in his conviction that man's happiness depends upon his character and not upon his circumstances, in his mistrust of the cold god, Reason, and his belief in the soundness of the intuitions of the heart, Vauvenargues stands alone among his compeers. He stands alone, too, among them in his personal nearness to Voltaire's affections. The noblest testimony to Vauvenargues' character is that it compelled the reverence of him who reverenced nothing; and the finest compliment ever paid to Voltaire was to be loved by a Vauvenargues.
Born on August 6, 1715, at Aix in Provence—in a mean house which still stands and is to-day a grocer's shop—Luc de Vauvenargues came of a poor family of provincial *noblesse* and was from the first what he remained to the last, delicate in constitution and with limited prospects of worldly success. His very imperfect education he received at the College of Aix, where his small Latin and less Greek were frequently interrupted by ill health. But he had a possession which is in itself an education—a good father.
Joseph de Clapiers had been created Marquis de Vauvenargues in 1722, when Luc was seven years old, for having been the only magistrate in Aix who did not run away from the place and his duty when a pestilence devastated the countryside in 1720.
For companions, Luc had two younger brothers and a cousin of his own age, a coarse, clever, selfish, undisciplined boy, named Victor Riquetti Mirabeau, who was to become the 'crabbed old Friend of Men' and the great father of a greater son. The boys had little in common but genius, and were attracted to each other by their very unlikeness. At sixteen, Luc was reading with passionate transport that 'splendid painting of virtue' 'Plutarch's Lives' (in a translation) and then the

letters of Brutus to Caesar, 'so filled with dignity, loftiness, passion, and courage,' said he, 'that I never could read them calmly.' Victor had already plunged into that blusterous, incontinent life which was to bring ruin to his own family and quite spoil the effect of his loud-voiced schemes for the good of mankind.

When both were seventeen the pair parted for a while. Luc must choose one of the only two professions open to his caste —the Church or the Army. The Church would not do, because, boy though he was, he was already philosopher and thinker—ay, in the noblest sense of the word—free-thinker too. Then it must be the Army! Picture this new subaltern of the King's Own Regiment, in the loveliest pale grey uniform, faced with Royal blue, with the most splendid braidings, and the very buttonholes sewn with gold silk, with his tall, boyish figure, his handsome face, his 'proud and pensive grace'—for all the world like the soldier-hero of a woman's novel. But he was already something very different from that. The handsome face bespoke a noble nature, ambitious for all great things, strong and ready to begin the world, to play his part therein if it be the part of a man of Deeds alone—or if the Deeds be but foundation for the Thoughts.

His first campaign was in Italy in 1733 with Marshal Villars, who was on his last. Italy! the land of dreams! The boy was filled with splendid visions of following Hannibal across the mountains—with young sanguine hopes of gloriously doing his duty and meeting immediate, glorious rewards. For three years he knew the intoxication—and the horrors—of a victorious campaign. And then of a sudden he found himself condemned at one-and-twenty to the vicious idleness, the low pleasures, and the deadening routine of a garrison life. The rich officers were of course drawn by that magnet, the Court, to keep up their military studies and prepare for the next war by dancing attendance on women and flattering the Minister and the King at Versailles. The poor ones remained on duty— with not enough of it to keep them out of mischief, and with, for the most part, debased tastes, because their intellectual limitations precluded them from higher.

The contamination of that useless existence even a Vauvenargues did not wholly escape. For a brief while he was as other men are. But the pleasures of a garrison town could not long hold such a nature as his. Already—he was but twenty-two—he had that love of solitude which, says a great German philosopher, is welcomed or avoided as a man's

IV: VAUVENARGUES: THE APHORIST

personal value is great or small. Already—at an age when other men scarcely realise they have a soul—this man was dominated by the idea of its value and dignity; and deep within him was the passion and resolution to exercise to the full its powers and possibilities.

With his companions he was wholly simple, natural, and friendly—without the faintest taint of that conscious superiority which makes many good people at once useless as a moral influence and objectionable as companions. 'Father,' his brother officers used to call him. Marmontel said 'he held all our souls in his hands.' He soon resumed, by correspondence, his friendship with Victor Mirabeau; and in their discussions on love—the view he takes of this passion is always a sure test of a man's character—each letter-writer showed the yawning gulf that divided him from the other.

If Vauvenargues ever met the woman worthy to hold his heart, to be, in the finest and highest understanding of those words, his companion and completion, is not known. He writes of love as if he had felt it. But to some pure souls—as to a Milton and a St. John the Divine—are revealed in visions the Eden and the New Jerusalem wherein they never walked. Vauvenargues' letters to Mirabeau treat of the subject with such an exquisite dignity and refinement—with such noble silences—that there is at least no doubt that if he never found the woman who would have realised his ideals, he was spared the bitterness of loving one who broke them.

Cousin Victor easily perceived that this thoughtful young soldier was fitted for something widely different from the life of a garrison town. Come up to Paris, then! Take up letters as a career! Win the smiles of the Court, and a pension from the Privy Purse! But Vauvenargues not only preferred literature to the sham called literary fame, but he loved his own profession. Thinker as nature had made him, thinker, moralist, aphorist as he has come down the ages, he was first of all a man of action, and so sound in thought because he was so strong in deeds. All his maxims were 'hewn from life.' When the death of the Emperor Charles VI in 1740 shook the kingdoms of Europe as a child shakes its marbles in a bag, Luc de Vauvenargues shouldered his knapsack and went out to Bohemia under the command of Belle-Isle. Ready to dare and to do, brave, young, high-spirited, knowing no career more glorious than arms, he looked round him and drew from keen experience his views of the world.

The philosopher in a study, weighing the *pros* and *cons* of motives he knows by hearsay, of deeds of which he has read, of passions he has never felt, may be a very fine thinker, but will hardly be chosen as a sound guide to practice.

The explorer who has faced the torrent and the mountain, the burning sun of the desert, hunger and cold and thirst, who has himself fought with beasts at Ephesus, will have a knowledge of the country he has discovered, which no books and lectures, no geographical or topographical knowledge can ever give to the cleverest student at home. The worth and the use of Vauvenargues' axioms on life lie largely in the fact that *he had been there himself.*

The very brief triumph of the capture of Prague in 1742 was succeeded by the horrors of the great mid-winter march from Prague to Egra. The King's Own suffered terribly. Death, defeat, famine, Vauvenargues knew not as names but as realities. In the spring of 1742 he had lost a young comrade, de Seytres, and wrote an *éloge* of him. Its immature and stilted style gives little idea of the warm feeling it clothed. Morley speaks of Vauvenargues' 'patient sweetness and equanimity' as a friend; and records how hardship made him 'not sour,' but wise and tender. All through that fearful march, in this strange soldier's knapsack were the manuscripts of 'Discourses on Fame and Pleasure,' 'Counsels to a Young Man,' and a 'Meditation on Faith.' Of many of his maxims on patience and the brave endurance of suffering, he must have found at this time cruel personal need.

The handsome young officer who had left France in the prime of his hopes and his manhood, returned to it with his health utterly ruined, both his legs frost-bitten, and his lungs seriously affected.

Still, he gathered together the strength he had left him and the pluck that never failed him, rejoined his regiment in Germany in 1743, fought nobly for his fallen cause at Dettingen, and returned to the garrison of Arras at the end of the year, an invalid for life.

It was now obvious he could no longer pursue his calling. Though he wrote with a keen and bitter truth that courage had come to be regarded as a popular delusion, patriotism as a prejudice, and that 'one sees in the army only disgust, *ennui*, neglect, murmuring; luxury and effeminacy have produced the same effrontery as peace; and those who should, from their position, arrest the progress of the evil, encourage it by their example,' yet still he would, if he could, have been soldier to the end. For a time he thought of diplomacy. 'Great positions soon teach great minds,' was one of his axioms. He would have been well fitted. But merit was not of the slightest help to advancement. To fawn on the King and the Mistress, to prostitute one's life and one's talents to a Court—here was the way to promotion. Vauvenargues wrote to the King and corresponded with Amelot the Minister, who answered most amiably and affably—and did nothing at all. 'Permit me, sir,' wrote Vauvenargues to him at last, with the directness taught in camps, 'to assure you that it is a moral impossibility for a gentleman, with nothing but zeal to commend him, ever to reach the King.' Amelot, stung a little, promised the next vacant post, and this time promised sincerely.

Vauvenargues retired to Provence and to quiet, to learn his new business. There he was attacked by confluent small-pox, which left him nearly blind and wholly disfigured: a misfortune he felt painfully as 'one of those accidents which prevent the soul from showing itself.' But worse than any disfigurement, the partial blindness made, of course, a diplomatic career an impossibility for ever.

Before the campaign of 1743, Vauvenargues had introduced himself to Arouet de Voltaire, by a letter in which the obscure soldier-critic compared Corneille disadvantageously with Racine. Nothing is so delightful in Voltaire's own genius as his generous recognition of other men's. Nothing is more to his honour than his high admiration for the moral gifts of a Vauvenargues who was young enough to be his son, who was poor, forlorn, a nobody, and whose fine qualities of lofty high-mindedness, delicacy, patience and serenity found, alas! no counterpart in Voltaire's own nature. It is so much the more to his credit that he could admire what he could never imitate, and appreciate what was wholly foreign to his temperament. He rejoiced in the thoughtful ability of that letter. 'It is the part of such a man as you,' he replied, 'to have preferences but no exclusions.'

The campaign of 1743 had interrupted their relationship. But they resumed it now, and, behold! it had turned into friendship.

Voltaire was at this time fifty years old, famous as the author of the 'English Letters,' the 'Henriade,' a few brilliant plays, and also as Court wit and versifier. But he was already in mental attitude what he had not yet become in mental output and in active deed. He could recognise in this Vauvenargues not only a friend and a literary critic, but a thinker and a philosopher. Vauvenargues sent him by degrees most of his writings, and Voltaire's criticisms thereon, as sincere as they were enthusiastic, were in themselves a powerful persuasion to the man of deeds to become man of words; while the Master's whole-hearted devotion to his own profession—the best and the noblest of all, though it bring no bread but the bread of affliction and of tears—was a further strong inducement to Vauvenargues to join the great brotherhood too. This soldier-thinker can tell men what to do when we have made them free to do what they will! He is, he has confessed it, as 'follement amoureux de la liberté' as I myself! To the individual soul he can give the help and the courage I have tried to give to the race, and to the riddle of the painful earth he can bring a wiser, tenderer, and braver solution than mine!

Vauvenargues was not, in fact, an intellect a Voltaire would lose. The young soldier decided to adopt literature as a profession, and began the world afresh.

Everything, save only Voltaire's encouragement, was against such a decision. The old Marquis de Vauvenargues—from a very natural but very mistaken and unrobust tenderness—would have kept his son at home to lead a safe, idle, invalid life in Provence, with a stroll on the terrace of the Vauvenargues' country-house for exercise, a thick-headed provincial neighbour for mental recreation, and his own aches and pains for an interest. His other relations (on the principle of Myrtle in 'The Conscious Lovers'—'We never had one of *our* Family before that descended from Persons that Did anything') objected to letters for one of Us as a low walk, leading directly to the Bastille. It *was* true that the moment was an inglorious one for literature. The Encyclopædia was unconceived. Voltaire himself was not yet the mighty influence he was to become. Writing *did* pay badly, and the young Marquis was deadly poor. Greatest objection of all was his own strong leaning to a life of action, and he himself first wrote of literature as being as 'repugnant' to him as to his family. 'But necessity knows no law.'

That momentary bitterness passed. 'Despair is the worst of faults,' said he. It was his part—allotted to him by misfortune, by fate, by God—no longer to act himself, but to teach other men how to act. He thrust aside the objections of his relatives. 'It is better to derogate from one's caste than from one's genius.' He silenced his own disappointment. 'A great soul loves to fight against ill fortune … and the battle pleases him, independently of the victory.'

IV: VAUVENARGUES: THE APHORIST

In May, 1745, he came up to Paris, and in a very humble lodging, where the Rue Larrey and the School of Medicine are now situated, began the world afresh.

Anyone who supposes his discontent to come from his circumstances and not from himself, should consider the life of Vauvenargues, and the one book with which he has enriched humanity.

Disappointed, disfigured, a failure; useless for the career he had loved, incapable of the career he had tried; cast off by his own people; solitary in a great city; often in pain of body, and because the work he had chosen was not the work Nature had originally chosen for him, often in pain of mind too—if ever man had an excuse for cursing God and fate, it was surely Luc de Vauvenargues.

La Rochefoucauld, rich and prosperous, with friends, position, and honour, had denied human virtue, and assailed it with cold malignities which still strike despair into the soul; and Voltaire himself, the most successful man of letters in history, turned upon life with gibes, and sneered at faith and happiness as alike chimæras.

But Vauvenargues looked out on the world which had given him nothing, with serene and patient eyes, and in a single book, as direct, strong, and simple as his own nature, evolved one of the most wise and comforting, one of the most sane, serene, and practical schemes of life, given to our race.

The great questions, Why am I? Whither go I? Whence came I? he asked himself as a thoughtful man must, but being a doer long before he was a thinker, he wasted little time in vainly seeking to answer them. Among his papers are a Prayer as well as the 'Meditation.' For simple faith he had ever reverence and envy—for all solemn questions a deep respect; and though he had no formulated religion, was yet deeply religious. But with him to be religious meant to Do Well. Live this life aright, and the next will take care of itself. 'The thought of death deceives us, it makes us forget to live: one must live as if one would never die.' To waste time and energy in idle discussion and speculation on another world when there is so much to do to set this one straight, found no countenance from this man of Deeds. Do, not dream, was his motto for ever.

There is not a page in his book—there is scarcely a line—which does not bear witness to his strong faith in men's honour and goodness, to his passionate conviction that out of worst evil one can get good, that the cruellest misfortunes ennoble and purify if one will let them, and our griefs may be for ever our gains. The hand that wrote was fevered with disease. No rich man, this, announcing glibly how comfortable it is to be poor. In the most vicious of all ages—and in not the least vicious of that age's environments—Vauvenargues had preserved his high ideals and his lofty character, and in sickness, sorrow, and disappointment he practised daily the courage he preached.

Instead of mockery—the besetting sin of his generation— this man, and this man alone, had for men's follies and absurdities only infinite compassion. Of him has been aptly quoted Bacon's beautiful phrase, 'he had an aspect as though he pitied men.' His philosophy remains for ever to the unquiet heart at once balm and tonic—the cool hand of compassion on the burning forehead—the touch of a friend, who knows—the strong grasp of help to raise the feeble from his weakness and despair, and to make him do what he can.

Some of the axioms have become part of men's speech, if not part of their soul.

'Great thoughts come from the heart.'

'We should comfort ourselves for not having fine talents, as we comfort ourselves for not having fine positions; we can be above both by the heart.'

'Great men undertake great things because they are great, and fools because they think them easy.'

'Would you say great things? Then first accustom yourself never to say false ones.'

'Who can bear all, can dare all.'

'Envy is confessed inferiority.'

'Few sorrows are without remedy: despair is more deceptive than hope.'

'Who gives his word lightly, breaks it.'

'He who has great feeling, knows much.'

'To the passions one owes the best things of the mind.'

Into that mad devotion to wit which was the snare of all his compeers, Vauvenargues never fell. He worshipped at the shrine of a diviner goddess called Truth. There is not a single example—even in his maxims, when the temptation would naturally be strongest—of his sacrificing fidelity to smartness. In February 1746, after he had been less than a year in Paris, he published anonymously that book by which he has gone down the ages and up to the gods, and which contains only the 'Introduction to the Knowledge of the Human Mind,' some 'Reflections,' the 'Counsels to a Young Man,' a few

IV: VAUVENARGUES: THE APHORIST

critical articles, the 'Meditation on Faith,' and the 'Maxims.' Clear, clean, and vigorous in style, as sharp and brief as a military order—it was well said by a friend that its author 'wanted first of all to get along quickly and drag little baggage after him;' and better said by himself that, 'when an idea will not bear a simple form of expression, it is the sign for rejecting it.'

It was not the sort of work likely to bring him present fame, or money. He did not expect them. As he worked in his miserable lodgings, ill lit and ill warmed, already a prey to consumption, and suffering often acutely from the old frost-bites—no such hopes had buoyed him. But he did what he had told other men to do—worked for the work's sake—and he found what he had told them they would find, joy in the working and satisfaction in a noble aim, be it unrewarded for ever.

The book dropped from the press perfectly stillborn. Reflections and moralities in the Paris of 1746! No, thank you. No one even troubled to abuse it. No one, except Marmontel, who was Vauvenargues' personal friend, reviewed it. But Voltaire loudly pronounced it one of the best books in the language: 'The age … is not worthy of you, but it has you, and I bless Nature. A year ago I said you were a great man, and you have betrayed my secret.' After Vauvenargues' death he wrote of him, 'How did you soar so high in this age of littleness?' and spoke of the 'Maxims' as characteristic of a profoundly sincere and thoughtful mind, wholly above all jealousies and party spirit. For sixty years the book lay germinating in a hard and barren soil, unworthy of it; and then rose fresh and strong from oblivion to the just and growing fame it enjoys to-day. It has been well said 'to give the soul of man an impetus towards truth.'

Though his tastes, his poverty, and his health alike precluded Vauvenargues from joining in the socialities of the cafés and the salons during his brief life in Paris, he saw sometimes Marmontel and d'Argental, and often Voltaire. Marmontel was still only a boy who had just started literary life on a capital of six louis and the patronage of Voltaire; and d'Argental, Voltaire's dear 'guardian angel,' was the nephew of Madame de Tencin, and, perhaps, the author of her novels. Marmontel was on a very different plane of intellect and character from Vauvenargues—while the one was a lusty boy beginning the world, the other was a patient thinker who was leaving it. But in those bare and dreary surroundings, in the disfigured invalid of whom men had never heard, even the commonplace cleverness of a Marmontel worshipped a hero. Long years after, he speaks of Vauvenargues' 'unalterable serenity'—of his brave and tender heart. 'With him one learnt to live and learnt to die.'

As for Voltaire, one can picture him just elected to the French Academy, the protégé of Madame de Pompadour, the dearest friend of young Frederick the Great, and fast becoming the most astonishing man in Europe, entering into the dull room, full of liveliness and animation, ay, and full too of real kindness and sympathy, while the invalid sat by the fireside listening silently awhile, and then striking across the Master's brilliant volubility with some quiet truth which he had long proved and pondered. That he found Voltaire's conversation a powerful stimulus to his own mind, and a very real delight, is not doubtful. There are few Voltaires in the world, and it was one of Vauvenargues' misfortunes that, save Victor Mirabeau, he had known scarcely anyone who was his intellectual equal. But if Voltaire roused the mind, Vauvenargues strengthened the soul. After his death, Voltaire wrote of him that he had always seen him 'the most unfortunate and the most tranquil of men.' It was this lucky genius of an Arouet who brought his fumings and his impatience, his irritableness over this, his chagrins about that, for the consolation of the man to whose sufferings his own had been as a drop in the ocean.

Vauvenargues always seems the elder of the two, as it were. He was as certainly the wiser, as he was certainly the far inferior genius.

What were his thoughts when those few friends had left him? It is on their testimony that he never uttered a complaining or a bitter word. His writings contain not an angry line—not one rebellion against God and Fate. It was the happy people who grumbled—perhaps it always is. Once, only once, there is a striving against destiny. In a moment of relaxation from bodily pain he wrote to an intimate friend, 'I have need of all your affection, my dear Saint-Vincens: all Provence is in arms, and I am here at my fireside.' He went on to offer his feeble help to the service he had loved, and to beg for the smallest post in his old active career.

But in a second came realisation. He was too ill to be of any use. Only thirty-two, he saw life slipping from him, and leaving him at that fireside a wreck, only fit for the hulks. But he bore 'his dark hour unseen,' and troubled no man with his troubles.

IV: VAUVENARGUES: THE APHORIST

His disease gained on him daily now. For the last year he was too ill to write. How far harder to die bravely by inches, unable even to do one's work, than to rush a smiling hero upon the swords in a glorious moment of exaltation, unweakened by disease, and uplifted by the applause of just men and of one's own heart!

Vauvenargues saw death coming slowly while it was yet a great way off, and was not afraid. No saint this, beholding in fervid ecstasy the vision of a world to come; but a strong man who had done his best with the world he had, and had written of that unknown future only in patient hope. 'My passions and thoughts die but to be born again: every night I die on my bed but to take again new strength and freshness: this experience of death reassures me against the decay and the dissolution of my body.'

He had lived to do his duty and to think of others, and thus he died.

The date was May 28, 1747, and the period one of the least honourable in the life of his friend Voltaire. But from his sycophancy of Pope and King, from a foul and noisy Court, from feverish bickerings with his Madame du Châtelet, and the coarse worldliness of his old Duchesse du Maine, Vauvenargues' death recalled him to his truer self, and roused him to the real work of his life. No other loss he ever suffered, it is said, affected him more profoundly.

If the fact that Vauvenargues loved him bears high testimony to the character of Voltaire, the virtue of Vauvenargues, like the virtue of Addison, may well give 'reputation to an age.' Flippant and false, at once supremely clever and supremely silly, the eighteenth century, to whom Duty was a mockery and Wit was a god, is in some sort redeemed by the brave, silent life, and the high ideals he proved practical and not visionary by fulfilling himself, of this soldier aphorist.

While of all the Brothers of Progress, Vauvenargues alone approached Truth as a suppliant, and thus gained, surely, the nearest vision of her face.

V: D'HOLBACH: THE HOST

In the most sociable city, in the most sociable age in the history of the world, there is one man who stands out as the host *par excellence*. In the Rue Royale at Paris and in his country house at Grandval, near Charenton, Baron d'Holbach entertained for more than thirty years the wit and the celebrity of all nations. His name runs like a thread through the English memoirs and letters of the mid-eighteenth century. There was not a Frenchman or a Frenchwoman of fame and fashion who had not dined at the Rue Royale on the immortal Thursdays and Sundays, or driven down from Paris to Grandval for a few days of a company and a conversation unequalled and, perhaps, unrivalled.
But it is not only or chiefly as the Host of All the World that d'Holbach is remarkable. He was the '*maître d'hôtel* of philosophy.' Voltaire, banned and exiled, could only encourage his children from lonely Cirey or far Geneva. D'Holbach was here, in the midst of them.
Comfortable, cultured, liberal, the freest of all free thinkers, and yet always in the smiling good favour of the authorities, not shy and retiring like d'Alembert, not wild and imprudent like Diderot, without a profession to distract him from his appointed metier, with a well-stocked mind, an enormous income, a fine library, a pretty wife, a first-rate cook, and an admirable cellar—why, here was the man intended by Fate to be the link to bind us together and to make for us a meeting-place, a common ground, where, in words to be first applied only to the Head of our Party,

> In very wantonness of childish mirth
> *We* puffed Bastilles, and thrones, and shrines away.
> Insulted Heaven, and liberated earth.
> Was it for good or evil? Who shall say?

* * *

Paul-Henri-Thiry d'Holbach was born in 1723 at Heidelsheim, in the Palatinate. His father, said Jean Jacques Rousseau when he had quarrelled with the son, was a *parvenu*. Another of Paul-Henri's guests announced that his host was called Baron because he was 'of German origin, had a small estate in Westphalia, and an income of sixty thousand livres.' Very little is known with certainty of his family. He was brought up in Paris, and was from the first French of the French, Parisian of the Parisians. He seems to have visited Germany as a very young man, and to have studied natural science there. He made his bow to the literary world by translating German scientific works into French. At his death Grimm wrote in the 'Literary Correspondence' that the rapid progress natural history and chemistry had made for thirty years in France was largely owing to the Baron d'Holbach.

As a young man the Baron was what he remained all his life — a compiler, an annotator, a transcriber, rather than the possessor of any great original talent of his own. Boy and man he had in perfection that gift which surely makes for human happiness more than any other single quality — a devoted love of learning. He was always rich enough to buy the books and the leisure to gratify that love. He lived in an age and in the midst of brilliantly accomplished men and women. He should have found life delightful. He did. A serene, easy, generous nature, troubled by no agitating ambitions, everything seems to have fallen out from the first according to his modest desires. For him, and for him alone among Voltaire's co-operators, the path to light and knowledge flowered pleasantly all the way. The others look out eagerly from their portraits — furrowed foreheads and burning eyes — or with faces noble and sad, like d'Alembert or Condorcet. Only the good Baron is seated at his ease in his pleasant, sumptuous garden, surveying life calmly and leisurely. Which things are a parable.

In 1752 or 1753, when he was about thirty years old, he began writing articles for that Encyclopædia which set on almost all its other contributors the ban of Government ill-favour. Only Paul-Henri — writing always judiciously under a pseudonym — gained nothing but pleasure and approbation from his excellent papers on mineralogy and chemistry. He formed the happiest life-long friendships with his fellow-writers in that immortal book. He married a pretty and charming wife, Mademoiselle d'Aine. She died, in August 1754, after a very brief married life. D'Holbach travelled abroad with Grimm for a while.

In 1755, he obtained a special dispensation from the Pope, and married his deceased wife's sister, Mademoiselle Charlotte-Suzanne d'Aine, and began to live with her a life which presented the very rare combination of perfect domestic contentment and the most brilliant social success.

In the very heart and core of Paris, Rue Royale *butte* Saint-Eoch, the Baron held in his town house what Rousseau calls the 'club holbachique,' Diderot 'the synagogue of the Rue Royale,' and Garat 'the Institute of France before there was one.' Here, at two o'clock every Sunday and Thursday, unless the d'Holbachs were in the country, their friends were certain to find a free and affluent hospitality, the most intellectual society of the capital, the most distinguished foreigners who visited it, a host as liberal in idea as in the very good cheer to which he made his guests welcome, and the most daring speculative conversation of the eighteenth century.

But, after all, it was not in the Rue Royale that d'Holbach and his friends found their most characteristic setting. Grandval, near Charenton, remains not only the most influential *salon* of the age, the great headquarters of a great party and the arsenal in which were forged the armaments which destroyed a king, a dynasty, and a state religion, but also *the* country house of the period.

When Talleyrand, in that much quoted phrase, declared that no one knew how delightful a thing life could be unless he had belonged to the upper classes before the Revolution, he might have been thinking of the life at Grandval in particular. There was a fine and charming *château*, and the most delightful of gardens. Grandval was just near enough to Paris, and just far enough away—which is to say, it was absolute country, within easy reach of town, in an age when the suburb was not, or, at least, when the social drawbacks comprehended in the word 'suburban' had no existence. The estate actually belonged to Madame d'Aine, d'Holbach's mother-in-law, who was as 'lively as any romp of fifteen,' always thoroughly enjoying herself, determined her guests should do the same, and with the rare wisdom to leave them to do it in their own way.

Madame d'Holbach was pretty, gay, and charming. She played on the lute, adored her husband and children, and hated philosophy. If her guests like to talk it—and they are always talking it—well, by all means, so they shall! Live and let live, do as you like come what may—these would have been the Grandval rules, if it had ever bothered itself to have anything so tiresome as rules.

The d'Holbach children were adorable—or despatched to governesses and servants if they even threatened to become less than adorable. There were two little boys and a couple of little girls, the elder 'as pretty as a cherub,' said Diderot, and the younger 'a ball of fat, all pink and white.'

Then there was an *ami de la maison*, a household fixture, a

V: D'HOLBACH: THE HOST

chimney-corner *habitué*—a Scotchman named Hope, and nicknamed Père Hoop—a shrivelled, withered, pessimistic person, who suffered, or said he suffered, from 'life-weariness' and bad health, who was an excellent foil to what Sterne called the 'joyous sett' in which he found himself, and the perpetual and dismally good-natured butt of Madame d'Aine's rippling jokes.

The Baron had all the virtues of the host. He was not only rich and generous—with that cook and cellar beyond reproach. In those days to be a perfect entertainer something more even than this was required. An agreeable talker, and a still more agreeable listener, really learned, but with the most pleasing human weakness for a little scandal, as easy-going as his mother-in-law and his wife, entirely simple in manner, with no faintest touch of pretension or affectation, a *bon vivant* in the pleasantest and most harmless sense of the phrase—who would not delight to have been among his guests?

There were generally three or four of them staying in the house, and sometimes very many more. Diderot was here often for weeks together, and sometimes for months. He had a special bedroom always reserved for him. In d'Holbach's most intimate confidence, his abundance, fecundity, and inspiration were in piquant contrast to the Baron's calm learning and well-regulated sense. Here too came, but not very often, Diderot's partner in the Encyclopædia, d'Alembert. Too shy and retiring to enjoy Grandval's freedom and liveliness as a recreation, d'Alembert's work for his party was not to be advanced, as his brethren certainly advanced their work, by speculative talk in clever company—but always in solitude, in silence, and in simplicity.

Turgot, like d'Alembert, was from time to time a guest, but a rare one. Turgot was beginning to Do, what most of his friends were still discussing How to do.

Little Galiani skipped down very often from the Italian Embassy, and the Paris he worshipped, to amuse the Baron's house-party by telling it those stories, 'like dramas,' which no one ever found too long. 'That man is a pantomime from his head to his feet,' said admiring Diderot, watching him. After 1761, the heavy Abbé Morellet, the would-be refuter of Galiani's wit on the Corn Laws, was constantly at the Baron's 'developing my theories on public economy' to his own great satisfaction. His audience have not left their feelings on record.

Grimm, Diderot's dear Damon, was here very often, with that

slightly nauseous affection for his Pythias, which, said the frankly vain Denis, made d'Holbach jealous. For jealous, one may be allowed to read 'disgusted.'
Grimm's *chère amie*, Madame d'Épinay, sometimes accompanied him. Her sister-in-law, Madame d'Houdetot, often drove down to Grandval with her superb Marquis de Saint-Lambert in her train. Pitted deeply with the smallpox, with a cast in her eye, and a little given to too much wine, the secret of Madame d'Houdetot's charm is hard to be found by this generation. But in that one, it was not only Rousseau who discovered it to his cost. Saint-Lambert's 'faith unfaithful kept him falsely true' to her for so many years that it came to be considered quite praiseworthy, and he would have been admitted to Grandval as Madame d'Houdetot's constant lover, if his passion for Madame du Châtelet and his poem on the 'Seasons' had not given him the *entrée* as a literary character as well.
His rival, Jean Jacques Rousseau, was also an *habitué* at d'Holbach's. The peaceful Baron could agree even with that fretful child of genius, until one unlucky day, when, Grandval having suffered gladly and politely a curé's reading of his own stupid tragedy, Jean Jacques bounces furiously out of his armchair, seizes the manuscript from its author, and throws it to the ground—'Do you not see these people are laughing at you? Go back to your curacy.' The kindliest and politest of hosts tries to smooth the ruffled plumage of both playwright and Rousseau. If the curé was appeased is not a matter of moment. Jean Jacques burst out of the house in a rage, and despite all the efforts of Grimm and of Diderot, as well as of d'Holbach himself, never returned to it. 'He imagined all his misfortunes our doing … and thought we had incited … all Europe against him,' says Grimm. He did try, however, to make some amends to his good host by portraying him in the 'New Éloïsa' in the character of Wolmar—'benevolent, active, patient, tranquil, friendly, and trustful.'
Marmontel came here very often: and that dreadful, garrulous old bore, the Abbé Raynal, was constantly to be found seeking ideas among the Baron's guests for his 'History of the Two Indies,' which received, and did not deserve, the advertisement of burning.
The cautious Buffon soon edged away from this *salon*, as he also edged away from the gatherings of Helvétius. The monstrous things these people talk about might come to the ears of the authorities—accompanied by the fact that the

politic author of the 'Natural History' was among the talkers! Helvétius himself was often at d'Holbach's, until the storm of fury and hatred which assailed his book 'On the Mind' banished him, astounded and embittered, to his estates in Burgundy.

Madame Geoffrin, with her prim little cap tied under her firm old chin, drove down to play picquet with the Baron and to scold Diderot for neglecting his wife.

It was partly owing to the influence of Diderot—himself greatly bitten by the Anglomania just creeping into fashion—that the Baron entertained Englishmen so largely both in Paris and in the country.

In the years 1762-64-66 Sterne accepted the hospitality of the host, whom he called 'the great protector of wits and the *sçavans* who are no wits,' to so large an extent that he could say the Baron's house was as his own. To be sure, d'Holbach's 'joyous sett' must have admirably suited this Parson Yorick, who had 'no religion but in appearance,' and a domestic morality very little better than the worst of the Baron's French *convives*.

The 'broad, unmeaning face' of Hume, the historian, was sometimes to be seen at d'Holbach's table, where he found himself for the first time with thinkers not too narrow, but too emancipated, for his liking. It was the Baron who, speaking from experience, warned Hume against nourishing in his bosom a serpent like Rousseau, and from d'Holbach's house, says Hume's biographer, Burton, that the story of the famous quarrel between Hume and Rousseau spread all over France 'in a moment.'

David Garrick came to Grandval, and delighted an age and a company passionately devoted to histrionic talent. A sprightly Madame Riccoboni used to write accounts of d'Holbach's society to the actor when he had gone back to England; and whenever she saw the Baron looked bored or worried, made that expression a text on which to moralise on the worthlessness of riches.

The Baron did not often appear anything but placid, however, and there are very few of his guests who even hint at anything in himself or his gatherings which was not smooth and delightful.

Horace Walpole, indeed, talks of 'dull d'Olbach's.' But then Horace was the intimate friend of Madame du Deffand, who loathed 'les philosophes' and all their ways and works, and on one occasion at least was so unlucky as to find himself at one of the Baron's dinner parties, not only the solitary Englishman out of a party of twelve, but next to that tedious Raynal. 'I dreaded opening my mouth in French before so many people and so many servants,' says Horace; and to avoid being bored by the 'Two Indies,' he made signs to Raynal that he was deaf. After dinner, Raynal discovered the trick, and naturally was not pleased.

John Wilkes, with his ugly face, his flaming past, and his irresistible charm, also sat at the Baron's cosmopolitan board; as did Benjamin Franklin, Lord Shelburne, and Priestley— Nonconformist, chemist, and one of the founders of modern scientific criticism.

Some of these people, of course, only dined, or were merely invited to spend a long day in the Grandval grounds and gardens; but many became part of the house party for days, like Galiani, for weeks, like Grimm, for months, like Diderot, or for ever, like Father Hoop.

In the forenoon, the guests were left entirely to their own devices, and unless by special arrangement, never met each other or their host until dinner-time at half-past one or two. Some of them had arrived with a *chef-d'oeuvre* in their pockets —or, it might be, up their sleeves. Here, in the pleasant solitude of these morning hours, Galiani, no doubt, was 'settling the question of the Corn Laws,' Grimm engrossed with his 'Literary Correspondence,' and Hoop arranging his pessimism into a regular system. (Madame d'Aine had thoughtfully provided Hoop with a bedroom overlooking the moat, so that he could at any moment put his principles into practice and throw himself into it.) Diderot, beside his open windows and with the solace of a cup of tea, wrote for Mademoiselle Volland those descriptions of life at Grandval to which all narrators of it are indebted.

As for the Baron—the Baron always seemed to have plenty to do in that magnificent library, where he could invariably find chapter and verse for the maddest of Diderot's theories, but where the actual nature of his occupation was known only to Diderot himself, to a certain very useful friend called Naigeon, who, having been painter and sculptor, had finally settled into a philosopher, and to La Grange, the d'Holbach children's tutor.

It is charitable to suppose that the women also performed their duties in the morning, since it is certain they performed none at any other time of day. But in this age, if a woman was witty and charming, her *métier* was considered to be fulfilled,

and she not only did nothing practical for the good of
humanity, but, better still, never even felt she ought to be
doing something. Madame d'Holbach had her lute and her
embroidery frame, the kindest of clever husbands, those
engaging babies, and a perpetual house party. What more
could be expected of her? Of Madame d'Aine, it is not
recorded that she had any other *rôle* than that of adding to the
gaiety of her household.
At about half-past one, then, the work of the day was done,
and hosts and guests met in the *salon*, and went in to dinner—
the famous dinner, exquisitely arranged and appointed;
servants numerous, noiseless, and perfectly *au fait* in their
duties; the most delicate wines, and the most irreproachable of
chefs. A couple of Englishmen, perhaps, and half a dozen
French men and women had driven down to it from Paris.
There were generally from twelve to fifteen persons at table,
and sometimes more. Good as the fare was—much too good
for the health of some of the diners—'the only intoxication' at
this table 'was of ideas.'
The talk ranged from the history and customs of the Chinese
to the final annihilation of the human race. Sometimes it lit on
'Clarissa Harlowe,' and the company divided itself into For
and Against Sentiment as understood by the bookseller
Richardson. Occasionally the meal was given up to
buffoonery, and Madame d'Aine led the way with jokes of
such a character that if Morellet is conscientious in declaring
in his 'Memoirs' that all freedoms, except freedoms as to
speculation, were banished from d'Holbach's gatherings, he
must certainly have been deaf. One day, a story going the
round of the Paris cafés, holds the table curious and laughing.
The Baron, says Grimm, was as amusingly credulous of gossip
as he was sceptical of everything else. Another day, it is a
question of *ton* or of *mode*; and a third, of art or of literature.
There was scarcely one of d'Holbach's *convives*—there was not
one of Voltaire's co-operators—who did not contribute, at one
time or another, a masterpiece, or at least a Book of the
Moment, for d'Holbach's table to discuss.
In 1755, it is the famous article on 'Existence' in the
Encyclopædia, by young Turgot, our shy, rare guest, which
brings the heads of the older Encyclopædists together over the
walnuts and the wine, and inspires them with prophecies of a
great future for its quiet author. Three or four years later, the
great suppression of that Encyclopædia itself inflames the
passions of the party, goads Diderot to fury, and d'Alembert

to despair.

In 1759, the 'Candide' of the Master sets the table in a roar of delight. 'The Social Contract' of our impossible, impassioned Jean Jacques sounds for us, in 1762, the trumpet-note of battle in that sonorous opening sentence: 'Man is born free, and is everywhere in chains.' The next year, the guests give their ever-generous admiration to a far wiser work—one of the mightiest weapons ever forged against 'the greatest of human curses'—'The Treatise on Tolerance.' In 1765, d'Alembert comes out of his shell again with his 'History of the Destruction of the Jesuits;' while Diderot is for ever finger deep in ink—up to the neck in ideas.

Only, at the head of the table, d'Holbach, host and president, always applauding, encouraging, (and sometimes also financing) the producers, himself produces nothing. Yet it is not because he does not go, as it were, with his guests. He goes far beyond them. Here, the women of the party left the table after dinner as they do in England, to exchange what Diderot called their 'little confidences.' Then the conversation took, not the kind of freedoms which Morellet declared he did not hear, but speculative liberties which, said he, 'would have brought down thunderbolts on the house a hundred times if they ever fell for that.'

At d'Holbach's table, with d'Holbach pushing, urging, with a quiet, invincible persistence, with Diderot waving the flag, leading, pleading, inciting, the 'club holbachique' dragged every dogma, every so-called fact of existence, every creed, into court before them; judged by the tribunal of their own reason, and cast away all that failed to satisfy it, as fagots for the burning.

Grandval did not speculate, as did Voltaire and his guests at Perney, on the attributes of God and the nature of the Soul. It began where he left off: asked not, What is God? but, Is there a God? not, What is the Soul? But, Have we a Soul? and in each case answered, No.

Gagged for hundreds of years, Grandval used the newly seized freedom of thought and speech as a very little later the mob used its social and political liberty. The bloody extremes of the Terror, and the speculative extremes of d'Holbach's table, were alike the result of long slavery and repression.

That d'Holbach at least was strongly and honestly persuaded of the truth of his own unbelief, and was convinced that he did well to destroy in men those faiths which, looking back on history, he saw were responsible for the intolerable miseries of religious persecution, is not doubtful. D'Holbach was an honest man. It is true, indeed, that he was not one of the highest intellectual capacity. His seems to have been just the kind of clever mind—much more common among women than men—which is the dupe of its own cleverness, and easily led by it into absurdities which both wise people, and very simple ones, detect and avoid.

Set the problem of deriving Everything from Nothing, it is not marvellous that the Grandval talkers descended sometimes to the wildest nonsense. Horace Walpole said acidly that they soon turned *his* head with 'a new system of antediluvian deluges which they have invented to prove the eternity of matter. ... Nonsense for nonsense, I prefer the Jesuits.' No wonder poor little Galiani (he *was* an Abbé, though he very often forgot it) fled to the more circumspect gatherings of Madame Geoffrin, that the wise Turgot also turned away from Grandval, and d'Alembert drew back from an atheism so positive and arrogant.

By the time the philosophers joined the women it was four, five, or even six o'clock. It *does* take some hours to construct Man and the Universe out of Chaos, with nothing but blind Force to help us! Then came for the host himself, and some few of the other men of the party, a walk in the beautiful gardens. Most of the Baron's guests, however, sat indoors with the women. Nature and exercise being both greatly out of fashion in the eighteenth century.

When the walkers returned the evening was drawing in, and there were lights and cards on the table. Some of the guests rested on long chairs. Some played picquet, some billiards, some tric-trac. Some visited their host's picture gallery or his famous cabinet of natural history. He was himself always pleasant, courteous, cheerful. He loved to rally gently 'the old mummy,' as he called Father Hoop, and, perhaps, other Fathers, certain Jesuit priests, whom, in defiance of all his own principles, he generously made free of his house.

Old Madame d'Aine entertained the whole company with her perfectly indecorous and perfectly good-natured wit. Madame d'Holbach, always 'douce et honnête,' 'très aimable,' and exquisitely dressed (the description is Madame d'Épinay's), accepted her mother's buffooneries with absolute complacency.

Coarse as this society was in its speech—worse as it was in its easy condonation of vice than the worst social sets of our own day—in one respect at least it was immeasurably superior.

Except for an occasional desultory game proposed by their hosts, the guests at Grandval were expected to bring, and did bring, their own entertainment with them in their own heads. To be bored would have been to confess oneself stupid. For the costly freaks of amusement, the elaborately idiotic devices of modern times to prevent the visitor having to fall back for an instant on his own resources or intelligence, Grandval had no need. If materialism was its creed, there was, as has been justly said, a great deal of 'indirect spiritualism' in its practice. Its lengthy dinners *were* feasts of reason (in spite of those intellectual extravagances) as well as of costly meats and wines, and the ill-flavoured jests were only interludes in the midst of brilliant and fruitful talk on literature, history, politics, and the new world beginning for France.

Supper came about nine—'wit, gaiety, and champagne,' Diderot described it. Then more conversation, until sometimes the party were still ardently philosophising with their bedroom candlesticks in their hands.

When d'Holbach had been entertaining, apparently without a break, for at least ten years, he took what seemed to his friends the foolhardy, not to say desperate, resolve of crossing the Channel. To bury himself in what Diderot called 'the depths of England' for two months is a very different thing, the Baron will find, from entertaining Englishmen (and those quite the most enlightened of their species) in Paris! He did find it so. If England delighted Voltaire, soothed wounded Helvétius, and pleased even critical Grimm, she thoroughly disgusted d'Holbach. He gave Diderot his vivid first impressions of her, and Diderot retailed them, red-hot, for Sophie Volland and for posterity.

The Baron was hospitably received and entertained in this island by a rich and generous host, whose name has not transpired; he had the best of health during his visit, and he paid that visit in August, when even the British climate can be very tolerable; he had the pleasure of calling on his guest, Garrick; he went to Oxford and Cambridge; travelled in some of the prettiest English counties, and he was bored—to extinction.

Our confessedly bad manners he found worse than anyone had ever found them before, and was dreadfully disgusted with people 'on whose faces one never sees friendliness, confidence, or gaiety, but which all wear the inscription, "What is there in common between you and me?"' The aristocracy struck him as cold and haughty, the common people as rough and violent. As for the dinner parties, 'where people sit according to their rank, and formality and ceremony are beside each guest,' after the gracious ease of Grandval, the Baron may be forgiven for finding them intolerable.

Then the public entertainments: 'This people is sad and melancholy, especially in places built for pleasure. You can hear a pin drop. A hundred stiff and silent women promenade round an orchestra discoursing the most delicious music,' and the promenade can only be compared to 'the processions of the Egyptians round the mausoleum of Osiris.'

Then the gambling: 'Englishmen lose incredible sums in perfect silence. By thirty they have exhausted all the pleasures, even beneficence. Ennui ... conducts them to the Thames, unless they prefer a pistol.'

At the universities, the good Baron found many 'rich do-nothings drinking and sleeping half the day;' at Court, corruption; among the people, no public education and great inequality of riches. The King, to be sure, was powerful chiefly to do good, but still lie was much the master. With regard to religion, 'the Christian religion,' said the Baron, 'is almost extinct in England.' This was an advantage from his point of view. But then, though there were innumerable Deists, like Hume, there was not an atheist, or not an avowed one. The travelling facilities he praised—there were always post-horses in plenty; and at the meals at inns, he found himself 'served promptly, but with no affability.' It must be owned that now and again the Baron has us on the hip.

But, after all, there was very great good in England: it made one so delighted to get back to France. D'Holbach, who had left Paris about August 1, 1765, had returned there by September 20. He dined that same evening with his dear Diderot and a whole colony of English, 'who had left their *morgue* and sadness on the banks of the Thames.'

Two years after his return, there appeared, not only to the horror of Court, Church, and Government, but to the horror of the philosophers also, a book called 'Christianity Unveiled, or an Examination of the Principles and Effects of Revealed Religion.'

It purported to be by a person called Boulanger. It asserted Christianity to be unnecessary for the maintenance of law and order; declared its dogmas incoherent, its morals fit only to make enthusiasts and fanatics, and its political results infinitely fatal and disastrous.

Voltaire fell upon the thing tooth and nail. 'Impiety Unveiled,' he called it. It was not Christianity, but the perversions of Christianity, with which he quarrelled. In the margin of his own copy of the book he wrote criticisms as scathing as they are brief. That it was both discussed and condemned at d'Holbach's table, is practically certain. Galiani at least professed Christianity; Turgot practised it. There are many men—there were some even round d'Holbach's board—who, having themselves relinquished a faith, are yet greatly averse to hearing that faith blasphemed; and who would fain leave for the souls of others the consolations their reason denies to their own. D'Holbach, to be sure, would commend the thing. 'A proselytising atheist,' as his friends had long known him to be—he *must* approve this daring effort to make men think as he did.

Soon came talk of other books—from the same hand it might be—certainly from a hand as bold. In 1767 appeared a pamphlet called 'The Mind of the Clergy;' in 1768 'Priests Unmasked,' and 'Portable Theology.' The last was condemned to be burnt.

Then came whispers of yet another work on the same lines, but on a far larger scale, written with an even greater daring, with 'the zeal of a missionary for atheism,' with a passion, a fanaticism, an enthusiasm, usually associated with the 'heated pulpiteer' of some narrow sect; and yet having in it, too, something of the serenity, the calm and confident faith of the believer wholly satisfied with his belief. Who has written it? A M. Mirabaud, Perpetual Secretary to the French Academy, is to be the name, it is said, on the title-page. But the real author? Diderot, whose Encyclopædic labours bring him in touch with all the literary men in Paris, is impulsively positive that he has not the slightest idea. Naigeon—Naigeon, the Baron's factotum—is abroad on some business of the Baron's and cannot be appealed to. Most of the company condemn the book unseen. The extremists of the party are always the worst enemies the party has to dread. At the head of his table, fingering his glass thoughtfully, the Baron, with his benevolent, leisurely air, is only following his usual custom in saying little and listening much.

In August 1770, there was published in London and Amsterdam 'The System of Nature, or The Laws of the Physical and Moral World,' by Mirabaud, Perpetual Secretary to the French Academy.

The best kept literary secret in history is the authorship of the

'Letters of Junius,' for that remains a secret still. But the Baron d'Holbach's authorship of 'The System of Nature' is certainly among the most piquant concealments in literature.

He had begun by sitting and listening to criticisms, mostly adverse, on his 'Christianity Unveiled' and the pamphlets which followed it, which were all from his pen. Many people start a literary career under as thick a veil of anonymity. A few have died still under the disguise. But no book has ever attracted such howls of rage and imprecation, such a storm of universal loathing and opprobrium as did 'The System of Nature,' while its author sat in perfect peace and comfort, beloved by all his fellows, safe, unsuspected, and serene. D'Holbach, said Grimm long after, when d'Holbach was dead and the secret out, never ran any danger from his books, save the danger of being bored by them.

Naigeon, La Grange, and Diderot were in his confidence. Diderot was more than in it. To most of the Baron's works—certainly to 'The System of Nature'—he lent some of the colour and fire of his genius. Poor Diderot was always suspect of anything rash and extreme. 'The System of Nature' was published quite early in August. On the 10th of that month, Denis slipped off to Langres and the baths of Bourbonne. The Baron went on having dinner parties. On the 18th, the book was condemned to be burnt. The Baron continued to dine in peace. Then, as men read it, and passed it secretly from one to the other, the murmurs of horror and hatred swelled to a roar —the roar of the great multitude, always deafening and terrible. Above it, d'Holbach heard, close, distinct, and scathing, the bitter condemnations of his own guests and friends. He went on dining to that accompaniment.

From Terney, Voltaire pronounced the work 'a philippic against God' and 'a sin against nature;' swore it had wrought irreparable harm to philosophy; passionately refuted it in his article on 'God' in the Philosophical Dictionary; while it wrung from him, in a letter to the Duc de Richelieu, that famous confession: '*I* think it very good to sustain the doctrine of the existence of a punishing and rewarding God: society has need of this opinion.' Galiani declared 'this Mirabaud' to be 'the Abbé Terrai of metaphysics: he causes the bankruptcy of knowledge, of happiness, and of the human mind.' La Harpe called it 'this infamous book.' Young Goethe said he fled from it as from a spectre. It caused Frederick the Great to break with the philosophic party. Grimm, indeed—but this was after d'Holbach's death, when it was no longer dangerous to hold such opinions—praised the purity of its author's intentions, and the passages of 'imposing eloquence' the book contained—though these, he added, Grimm-like, 'were by Diderot.'

Who reads 'The System of Nature' now? It never was in any sense a great book. But it certainly was one of the three or four most famous books of an age richer in them than any other age in history. It was, after all, simply the logical outcome, the natural, though the extreme result of the rationalistic criticism of the fifty or sixty years which preceded it. The philosophers had sought to define God. D'Holbach said aloud, what the fool of David's time said in his heart, 'THERE IS NO GOD.'

In Part I he disposed of Kings as effete, luxurious, war-making, and tyrannical. Then he expounded his views on Happiness. Men will never be happy till they are enlightened, and never enlightened till they have ceased to believe in a God. Study Nature, and obey Nature's laws—that is the way to felicity, if way there be. Then he went on to Mind. All Mind is Matter. Of Free Will he denied the existence, as twelve years earlier his friend Helvétius had denied it in his book 'On the Mind.' Still, even if one cannot help one's wrong-doing, punishments there must be, for the good of society; only such punishments should be reformative and never cruel. In his protest against torture and the brutalising effect of public executions, one sees for a moment the man behind the book. With regard to the Immortality of the Soul, since there is no such thing as soul, it cannot be immortal. The false doctrine of Hell is useless even as a deterrent from sin.

Part II contains what is certainly the most burning and outspoken attack on the Existence of God to be found in literature. That there is a Force behind Matter, I admit. He who does not admit this, must be a madman. But further I will not go. As for morality depending on a belief in a Deity—not at all. Nature bids man do right as his own best interest. Let each try to do his utmost for the greatest good of the greatest number, and there stands established a high and an unselfish ideal.

Preached, as these doctrines were, in a style not a little vehement and abundant, with much Teutonic pomposity and rhetoric, it could soon be said of d'Holbach that he had 'accommodated atheism to chambermaids and to hairdressers.' More learned critics disliked his manner as much as his matter. 'Four times too many words in the book,' says Voltaire acidly. But the uneducated, or the half-educated, prefer both their oratory and their literature rich and fruity. Simple and learned alike would, or should, had they known him, have given the author credit for the certain fact that 'no sordid end, no personal consideration, attached him to his dismal system.' If his anonymity shielded him from danger, it kept from him fame and celebrity too, and gave him the wholesome, but not soothing, experience of hearing expressed to his face criticisms of the kind generally only made behind one's back. He did not gain even the painful glories of martyrdom; and had money been an object to him, by the publication of such works as his, he can only have lost it. Long before the tumult 'The System of Nature' raised had passed away, the Baron was busy supplementing it. In 1772 appeared 'Good Sense, or Natural Ideas opposed to Supernatural Ideas,' which was a sort of simplification of 'The System of Nature.' It was burnt. Then appeared 'The Social System,' which tried to establish a rule of morality totally unfounded on religion. That was burnt too. Then there was a translation from Hobbes. The last, or one of the last, of d'Holbach's published works was entitled 'Universal Morality, or the Duties of Man founded on his Nature.' This appeared in 1776. He had the pleasure of watching all the bonfires from a distance where there was not the least danger of scorching.

In 1781 one of his daughters was married. Her father was now fifty-eight years old. Did philosophy, as Galiani inquired (Galiani had returned to Italy in 1769), still eat at his table with its old appetite? Grimm said—in Grimm's caustic fashion—that the guests fell off somewhat when the Baron had to retrench his expenses to establish his children. Some of the *convives* had gone before that, to solve for themselves those questions on a future world, and the existence of the soul, which they had discussed so often. In 1771 died Helvétius; in 1778 Voltaire himself. In 1783, d'Alembert, who had indeed long ceased to frequent the Baron's society, or any society, laid down the burden of his life. In the next year, Diderot, the friend of his heart, the fruitful inspiration of his work, was called away from d'Holbach's side for ever.

It must have been with this society, as it is with all societies at last: the sight of vacant chairs stops the mirth, and among the living guests glide others, dear and dead. When one has more memories than hopes, the time has come to give up such gatherings. That time came even to *the* Host of his generation. By his own fireside he had to the end the wife he loved. She long survived him. He had, too, that tranquil and even disposition which is surely one of the best of assets—a possession indeed.

The Baron was as prudent in the time of his death as he had been in the conduct of his life. He died on January 21 of that *annus mirabilis*, 1789. Five years more, and he would have seen his own principles enthroned with the Goddess of Reason at Notre-Dame, and as, in part at least, the consequence of her reign, the streets of Paris running with blood. Directly after his death, the secret of his authorship became public property.

It is permissible only to think of d'Holbach now as his guests and friends thought of him in life—not as the author of 'The System of Nature' at all, but as the liberal patron of letters, the best and kindliest of good, easy men. One may be permitted to hate as bitterly as Voltaire did the unreasonableness of his philosophy of pure reason; and yet to regard the philosopher with gratitude and appreciation, as the man who played in the great intellectual revival of his time one of the homeliest, yet one of the most necessary of parts.

For d'Holbach provided the *rendez-vous*.

VI: GRIMM: THE JOURNALIST

The great Encyclopædia of Diderot and d'Alembert was to bring light to the people; the 'Literary Correspondence' of Melchior Grimm was to bring light to kings. The Encyclopædia was the conception of those who knew that they were preparing mighty changes, but who did not live to see them; the 'Literary Correspondence' was the work of a man whose shrewd eyes foresaw little, but who lived to see all. The Encyclopædia is dead, as a great man dies, having finished his work. The 'Correspondence'—which could not cure those royal maladies, blindness, ignorance, and hardness of heart—still lives a gay little life as the most perfect contemporary record of any literary epoch in history.

* * *

In 1753, the sensibilities of sentimental Paris were most agreeably touched by the pathetic story of a young gentleman who, having had his suit rejected by a charming opera-dancer, Mademoiselle Fel, straightway took to his bed and to a trance in which he passed whole nights and days, 'without speaking, hearing, or answering, as if he were dead.' The Abbé Raynal and Jean Jacques Rousseau constituted themselves his nurses. They were both too romantic, and too much the children of their time, to try the common-sense expedient of leaving the rejected lover severely alone, or of throwing a bucket of cold water over him. But when Rousseau saw a smile on the doctor's face as he left the patient's room, his heart began to harden a little. And, sure enough, one fine morning up gets the invalid, dresses, resumes his ordinary course of life and never again mentions his malady to his nurses—even to thank them.

Frédéric Melchior Grimm was, however, no sentimental fool. He was, indeed, one of the most keen-witted of his great nation, though, like many other children of the Fatherland, he had on the surface of his worldly wisdom a fine layer of Teutonic sentimentality. If the Briton finds the sentiment mawkish, not so the Frenchman. Grimm's extraordinary disease became his passport into the most exclusive circles in Paris.

Born at Eatisbon on September 26, 1723, with a poor Lutheran pastor for a father, he had always known that he must make his own way in life, and had always made it. At school he found a useful friend in one of Baron Schomberg's sons, and continued the friendship at the University of Leipzig. When he was still a student there, he wrote a play, 'Banise,' which, before he left, he was a sufficiently just and astute critic to find 'pitiable.' On leaving Leipzig he went to live in the Schombergs' house, as tutor to his friend's younger brother. Frederick the Great had already made the French language the fashion; and as at the Schombergs' Grimm heard nothing else, he soon learnt to speak and read it. In 1748 came the first opportunity of his life; he took his pupil to Paris, and remained there after the boy had returned to his family.

To say that Grimm throughout his existence always fell on his feet, would be a misleading idiom. He always fell on his head. The moment he found himself thrown into a new set of circumstances, his calm judgment skilfully arranged them to the very best advantage. At this time he was twenty-five years old, rather tall and imposing looking, something of a dandy in his dress (his enemies declared that he powdered his face and scented himself like a woman), with very little money in hand, no prospects, and a retrospect of that dismal failure 'Banise,' and that 'thin travelling tutorship.' In a very short time he got himself appointed as reader to the Duke of Saxe-Gotha. The salary was thin enough here too; but the Duke was a great person, and the Duchess was the friend and the correspondent of Voltaire, and to be, for the rest of her life, the friend and correspondent of Melchior Grimm as well. He was not long in finding a situation much more lucrative and responsible.

In 1749, he became secretary, guide, and friend to a certain dissipated young dog of a Comte de Frise, or Frisen, who was always borrowing money of his famous uncle, Marshal Saxe, and certainly needed a prudent Grimm to look after him.

If Grimm was only, or principally, honest because honesty is the best policy, if he did his duty because in the long run duty is the surest road to happiness, yet the facts remain that he did act uprightly, and that he had settled principles, a strict course of conduct and a strong line of action, in an age when no motives, good, bad, or indifferent, produced such happy results in his friends.

Beneath that veneer of German emotionalism he was, perhaps, something cold and selfish, stern and reserved. But if he was never ardent, he was always faithful; if he was not generous, he was just. He occupied in his life many positions of great trust and responsibility, and came out of them all with honour. One can love a Diderot, but one must needs respect a Grimm.

He had plenty of work to do in Paris. Besides the impossible task of keeping Frisen in order, he had his own way and fortune to make and his own friends to cultivate. His passion for Mademoiselle Fel was not his only introduction to Parisian society. Jean Jacques Rousseau (then a brilliant pauper copying music for his support and dreaming masterpieces of which he had not yet written a line) introduced him to d'Holbach and to Madame d'Épinay. He soon became fast friends with Madame Geoffrin (to whose tranquil common-sense his judicious and well-ordered mind particularly appealed), with Helvétius, and with Marmontel; he began a life-long friendship with Diderot, and once a week at Frisen's house, in the Faubourg St. Honoré, he gave the most delightful bachelor dinner to his friends, played exquisitely on the clavecin for their benefit, took their amusement at his German-French in perfectly good part, and was entirely witty and agreeable, while keeping always a certain reserve and remaining entirely master of the situation.

In a very short time the poor German tutor was one of the most sought after persons in Paris, fêted and petted by all the great people, and minded to live no longer as bear-leader to boys, but by his own head and pen.

His taste for music gave him a golden opportunity. Shall we have French music at the opera, or Italian? Paris was as hotly divided on the question, said Rousseau, as if the affair had been one of religion. The French side had all the money, the fashion, and the women, and the Italian side a very little party of real connoisseurs. Grimm joined the Italians and wrote on their behalf, in 1753, a pamphlet called 'The Little Prophet of Boehmischbroda,' in which the style is profanely imitated from the prophets of the Old Testament. As Madame de Pompadour was on the French side, which she protected by force and by summarily dismissing the Italian singers on the spot, the pamphlet did no harm to French music; but it made Grimm famous. Voltaire read it, and asked how this Bohemian dares to have more wit than We have? And this Bohemian, having made so successful a literary venture in a small part, now looked round with his clever eyes for a larger one.

In 1754, he travelled for a time with d'Holbach, who had just lost his wife; and in the following year Frisen, whom Grimm's guardianship had not been able to save from the fatal consequences of his depravity, died, and left his mentor a free man.

In 1755 he began what was to be the work of his life and is his true title to glory, the 'Literary Correspondence.'

The idea of communicating to the sovereigns of Europe by letter, news of the literature, science, and philosophy of Paris, that centre of the world's cultivation, was not a new one. In limiting the freedom of the press, sovereigns had limited their own freedom. Newspapers were official bulletins, not daring to utter unacceptable truths or unpalatable opinions on any truths. Kings, as well as their subjects, yawned over journals of this kind. So King Frederick the Great originated the idea of paying an intelligent man in Paris to write him direct the news and the gossip of the capital. Theriot, Voltaire's friend, filled the post very unsuccessfully, and Frederick complained bitterly that Theriot never had a cold in his head without scribbling four pages of rodomontade to tell him about it. La Harpe occupied the same position to the Czarevitch Paul, and Suard and the Abbé Raynal, Grimm's nurse and friend, to the Duchess of Saxe-Gotha.

The idea was good, but it had been badly worked out. As Diderot and d'Alembert quickened into mighty life the little Encyclopædia of Chambers, so Grimm breathed vitality into the languishing 'Literary Correspondence.' He saw in it, first of all, the germ of a great career; but he saw in it, too, an influence which, by informing the minds of kings, might change the destiny of kingdoms. To teach the people was difficult in those days; to teach their rulers was well nigh impossible. Here, then, was a chance, the one splendid chance, of showing them the progress of the world, the ominous advance of knowledge and of the old order towards the new. Raynal handed over to Grimm the correspondence he had established with the Courts of the north and south of Germany; and with this small connection Grimm began his work.

The 'Literary Correspondence' remains to-day the only literary review which has survived the passage of time, and is still not merely a great name, but a great living work. The 'Spectator' and the 'Tatler' of Addison and Steele are kept eternally fresh by an exquisite charm of style; but they rarely aspired to serious criticism, and are mainly a record of modes and manners, not of literature or of science. The 'Literary Correspondence' is as much to-day as on the day it was written, the guide-book to the letters, the art, and the drama of the eighteenth century; the open door to its society and to the mind of cultivated Paris; a book which is equally indispensable to the scholar or to the novelist writing of its period, and which is certainly both the most instructive and the most amusing literary compilation extant.

Of no settled length and in manuscript, it was despatched to its subscribers twice a month. It had no fixed price, its readers paying as much as they chose for it, or as much as Grimm could make them pay. His old friend the Duchess of Saxe-Gotha was, as has been seen, one of his first subscribers. The Landgrave of Hesse, the Queen of Sweden, and Catherine the Great of Russia soon joined his select and limited *clientèle*. Stanislas Augustus, King of Poland, the Margrave of Anspach, and the Grand Duke of Tuscany joined later. Frederick the Great, after his unlucky experience with Theriot, was extremely dilatory and vacillating in having anything to do with it; when he did add his name to the list of subscribers he never paid his subscription and harried Grimm to insert the scandals and the *on dits* of the *cafés* and the Court, which Grimm declined to do.

For greater security, the sheets did not go through the post, but through the legations of the various countries. The thing was, in fact, a secret, and a well-kept secret, for more than half a century, and never knew the danger of print until it was published in 1812, under the Empire, with many cautious Napoleonic omissions. In the meantime, its secrecy and the limited number of its readers gave the discreet Grimm, who declared that the most enlightened reasoning was not worth a night in the Bastille, and who was cautious to the very fibre of his bones, the opportunity of being at once candid, impartial, and safe.

He set forth a flaming prospectus, promising an 'unlimited truthfulness.' The sheets shall be 'dedicated to confidence and frankness!' They were. To those distant Courts and Kings there went forth every fortnight the inimitable criticisms of the most bold, just, and cool critic who ever breathed. He not only analysed, with extraordinary brilliancy and fairness, the writings of Voltaire, of friend Rousseau, and of Buffon, but he sat in discerning judgment on the works of English novelists and poets. He criticised books which have not lived, in criticisms which are undying. As to the value and the longevity of the productions, he was sometimes, naturally and inevitably, mistaken; but as a rule his opinions have been confirmed by posterity and have weathered the test of time. He also described to his readers the condition of the drama, the plots of the plays, the art of the players. Of course he was clever enough if the season was rather a dull one, to fill out his pages with extracts from a tragedy or from a novel; sometimes, it is said, the ingenious man gave quotations from works which had never been written.

He dealt with medical questions, and did not think it beneath his dignity to examine the merits of a mouth-wash. He wrote many pages on Tronchin, the great physician, and on inoculation. Here, surely, was one of the chances to enlighten kings—kings who, more than any other class of men, suffered and died from the ignorant tyranny of their physicians, and who had to wait eighteen centuries before any man told them that fresh air was a valuable property, and health a kingdom to be taken by temperance, soberness, and chastity.

If there was a scientific marvel in the air, such as ventriloquism, why, of course, Grimm must tell his correspondents about that; and the music, French or Italian, of the capital, must also receive its comment. Then there was the news of the day, and of Academical disputes, and, though Grimm had declared he would not report them, occasional piquant anecdotes with a sufficient spice of scandal in them to have pleased King Frederick.

He further drew pen-portraits of celebrities. Nothing could be more fair and shrewd than Grimm's characters-ketches. He solves in them the supreme difficulty—how to be at once honest and charitable.

Next there is an epigram to be reported. While a charade that has amused a Parisian fine lady is surely good enough for a German duchess!

Politics were supposed to be excluded, and they were excluded in the sense that there were no remarks on public events until those events had become so notorious that the 'Correspondence' did not add to its readers' knowledge of them. But though, or because, he wrote for governors, Grimm adduced his theories on government, he himself believing in the divine rights neither of the 'Social Contract' nor of kings. To his views on tolerance, finance, and education, he gave utterance soberly, thoughtfully, and at length. He had a subscription list in his paper for Voltaire's unfortunate protégés, the Calas; and if his pen was to flow freely, as he had promised, how could he stay his indignation against the trial and the sacrifice of the Chevalier de la Barre?

To the friend and intimate of the philosophers, the most ordinary event suggested philosophical reflections. His religious views could hardly help appearing; but Grimm's was a quiet agnosticism, and had nothing in common with the excited certainties of Diderot's unbelief. He had, of course, his theories on women, on art, and on languages; and he aired them all. He brought out, in the same tantalising fashion in which serials are now produced in weekly illustrated newspapers, Diderot's two novels.

He was himself not only the first critic of his day, but he was thinker as well as chronicler, worldling and scholar, reporter and *savant*. Foreigner though he was, he had learnt to write the French language in a style inimitably clear, supple, and forcible. His command of irony alone should have been a fortune to him. Add to this, his singularly wise, calm head, and his unrivalled position as the friend of the women of the salons and the nobility of Paris as well as of its writers and politicians. Further, this critic of music was himself a musician, this judge of authors himself an author. He lived in one of the most momentous and thrilling periods in the history of this earth, and in one of the most stimulating of her cities, and was able to write wholly without fear of consequence for readers of whose intelligent interest he was sure, while he had ever before him the magnificent hope of so opening the hearts and feeding the knowledge of those readers that they might turn and do good unto their people and be a blessing, and not a curse, to their lands.

Consider all this, and it is not marvellous that Grimm remains the first journalist and the 'Literary Correspondence' the first newspaper in the world.

It is hardly necessary to say that it gave its editor an enormous amount of work. *Chaise de paille*, his friends called him in allusion to his diligence; later, when he began to travel, Grimm suggested the nickname should be altered to *chaise de poste*. He had many secretaries working under him. One, Meister, was attached to him all his life, and benefited largely under his will. When he was away from Paris the good-natured Diderot made a brilliant substitute; and Madame d'Épinay took up a delicate pen to become the first, and surely the most charming, of women journalists.

Only a few months after his arrival in Paris Grimm had been introduced to this little black-eyed, bright-witted, and all too seductive wife of a worthless husband. In 1752, at Frisen's table, he had heard her name insulted, and had fought a duel for its honour. By 1755, on his return from his journey with d'Holbach, he became a familiar figure in her salon. First her wise and masterful friend, he was soon her despotic lover.

It is always a vexed point of morals to determine how far right can come out of wrong, how far a cause initially bad can be said to be good in its results. It must certainly be conceded in Grimm's case that, having put himself into a false position and remaining there, he acted not only sensibly and discreetly, but even honestly and conscientiously. He found Madame d'Épinay silly, as are so many clever women, and he insisted on her behaving with judgment and discretion. One of his first acts was to demand that her old lover, Francueil, whom she still permitted to visit her as a friend, should be given his dismissal. With Duclos, man of letters, and of character rough, dissipated, and unscrupulous, he bade her break entirely. Then he turned to Rousseau.

It has been justly said of Grimm that he never lost a friend save Jean Jacques. In 1756 Madame d'Épinay, acting on one of those excessively foolish impulses which she herself felt to be wholly fascinating, and which had already more than once shipwrecked her life, gave Rousseau the little Hermitage in the forest of Montmorency, close to her own country-house of La Chevrette.

Grimm had not known Rousseau for six years without knowing his heart. He looked up suddenly from the 'Correspondence.' 'You have done Rousseau a bad service,' he told Madame d'Épinay sternly, 'and yourself a worse.' Still, it was done. In 1757, that *belle laide*, Madame d'Houdetot, also had a house close to La Chevrette, and there attracted the notice of Rousseau. After a brief summer day of delight, she grew tired of her vehement admirer, or her lover, Saint-Lambert, grew tired of him for her. At any rate, there burst over those three houses in the Montmorency forest a storm of fierce passions and scandalous recriminations. All Paris stood watching. Diderot plunged impulsively into that angry sea. Rousseau accused Madame d'Épinay, in terms which no self-respecting woman could have forgiven, of being the writer of a certain fatal anonymous letter; and she forgave him. Grimm had been appointed secretary to the Duke of Orleans, and was absent on duty in Westphalia. He did not spare his little mistress's pusillanimous weakness. 'Your excuses are feeble … you have committed a very great fault,' he wrote. Hurrying home, he dealt with Rousseau in terms of unmistakable plainness. He made Madame d'Épinay cast him off there, at once, and for ever, and carried her off to Geneva on the excuse, a just excuse in every sense, of her health.

But the consequences of her folly were not ended. Rousseau

defamed her character in the 'Confessions,' and in that unique masterpiece of scurrility he speaks of Grimm as 'a tiger whose fury increases daily.' Diderot declared that Jean Jacques made him believe in the existence of the devil and of hell. But Grimm wrote an obituary notice of Rousseau in his 'Correspondence' of admirable justice and moderation, and spoke of him as 'embittered by sorrows which were of his own making but not the less real,' and as 'a soul at once too weak and too strong to bear quietly the burden of life.' It must be allowed that Grimm could be magnanimous.

Having saved Madame d'Épinay from her friends, it remained to him to save her from herself. At Geneva he put her under the care of the great and good Tronchin, and made her write for the 'Correspondence.' He helped her to manage the miserable remains of the fortune her husband's mad extravagance had left her, supervised the education of her children, and even showed her the harm she did them by speaking disrespectfully of their father. His love was not fervent, perhaps, but it corrected her follies and her weakness, and made her do and be her best. It had at least some of the tokens of a good and honourable feeling.

These visits to Geneva were undoubtedly the happiest time in her life. On this first one, which lasted eight months, from February to October 1759, she and Grimm often saw and talked with Voltaire; and Grimm greatly appreciated the society of the solid and sensible Genevans and the cultivated Tronchins. Mademoiselle Fel came to stay with Voltaire at Les Delices, and when Grimm saw her there he proved convincingly the truth that 'the man's love, once gone, never returns.' But his real passion was not even for Madame d'Épinay. His dominant taste was his ambition; his dearest mistress, his career.

Already secretary to the Duke of Orleans, on the last evening of his stay at Geneva, he heard the satisfactory news that he was made Envoy for Frankfort at the Court of France. True, M. l'Ambassadeur, as Diderot called him, soon lost his post by joking in a despatch at the expense of an official person; but none the less he was rising in the world. Presently he was busy settling M. d'Épinay's bankruptcy and helping Madame to arrange a satisfactory marriage for her daughter. *Tyran le Blanc* he was called by her and her circle. But, after all, no woman is happy till she has met her master. Well for her if she find one as judicious and upright as Melchior Grimm.

He was less with her as the years went by, though not in any sense less faithful. In 1762 the Duchess of Saxe-Gotha appointed him her *chargé d'affaires*; and when she died her husband made him Councillor of Legation, with a pension. He met Frederick the Great when he was travelling in Germany in 1769; and Frederick, forgetting his grievance that Grimm would not turn the 'Correspondence' into a scandalous society newspaper, fell under the spell of his fellow-countryman's encyclopedical knowledge and dignified affability. Grimm, said Meister, had the rare talent of living with great people without losing any of the freedom and independence of his character.

When he was nearly fifty years old, in 1771, he resumed an employment of his youth, and, at a very large salary, consented to be tutor to the Hereditary Prince of Hesse, a boy about nineteen. The pair went to England and were well received at its ultra-German Court. Grimm was delighted with 'the simplicity, the naturalness, and the good sense' of the English character. The Landgravine, young Hesse's mother, sold her diamonds that her son might prolong his visit in so delightful a country. And then Grimm brought him back to Paris and formed his mind and manners in the society of d'Holbach and Diderot, of Madame Necker and Madame Geoffrin.

In 1773, tutor and pupil went to St. Petersburg to attend the marriage of Wilhelmina, the Prince of Hesse's sister, with the Czarevitch Paul. In a very short time the skilful Grimm had gained the great Catherine's interest and consideration. Even Diderot's warm heart and glowing genius (he was staying at the Russian Court when Grimm arrived there) did not win her so well as the German's delicate tact and keen perceptions. Herself before all things a great statesman, how should she not respect the shrewd judgment, the strength, and the determination of a Grimm? It is so rare to be clever and wise! It was most rare in the eighteenth century. Two or three times a week Grimm dined with her Majesty *en petit comité*—those dinners at which all men were equal, and at which no servants appeared to hamper the conversation. Afterwards she talked alone with him by the hour together. He told Madame Geoffrin how, when he left her, he would pace his room all night with the splendid ideas she had suggested coursing through his sleepless brain: 'The winter of 1773-74 passed for me,' he said, *'en ivresse continuelle.'* But when Catherine would have permanently attached him to her service, his stern good sense helped him to refuse. There is no such dead-weight on genius as a post at Court—be it the Court of a Catherine or a Frederick—and Grimm knew it. 'I have never seen you hesitate about anything,' Madame d'Épinay had once written to him; 'when you have once decided with your just, strong mind, it is for ever.'

His refusal was unalterable, and he returned to Paris. He was sure enough of his firmness to visit his royal friend again, two years later, in 1776. He had been acting tutor once more, to the two Counts Romanzoff this time. He had taken them to Naples to embrace Galiani, to Ferney to see Voltaire, and to Berlin to see Frederick. They arrived in Petersburg in time for the second marriage of the Czarevitch, of whose first marriage, with Wilhelmina of Hesse, Grimm had been the principal promoter. Catherine received him with the same flattering interest and offers, but he was as deaf to them as before. Then she gave him the title of Colonel—to the intense amusement of King Frederick—and appointed him her general agent in Paris at a salary of ten thousand livres.

After his return to the capital this appointment formed a very large occupation in his life.

His frequent absences had naturally not been the best thing in the world for the 'Literary Correspondence,' but it would have been a much worse thing if Diderot—Grimm's 'patient milch-cow whom he can milk an essay from or a volume from when he lists'—had not been there to do his work. The 'Correspondence' rightly appears with Diderot's name as well as Grimm's on its title-page. In these latter years, indeed, its readers often had to be content, not with Diderot, but with a mere Meister; and when Grimm did write himself it was sometimes carelessly and in a hurry. Not quite the first, or the last, perhaps, to commit that literary enormity, he occasionally reviewed books he had not taken the trouble to read.

His letters to and from Catherine, after the first few years, were not conveyed through the post, but by special messenger, and are therefore delightfully outspoken. Grimm's contain indeed a good deal of flattery and exaggeration; but Catherine's are spontaneous enough. She used to say she was as 'frankly an original as the most determined Englishman.' The pair wrote sometimes in French and sometimes in German. They had nicknames for most of the crowned heads in Europe. Of 'Brother George of England' Catherine had always spoken with contempt, and considered his loss of the American colonies as 'a State treason.' But much of the correspondence was devoted to mere homely details. As her agent, Grimm bought the imperial rouge for the imperial cheeks, pictures, books, and bon-bons. He took long journeys in her interest: he supplied her with architects when she caught a fever for building; and presently, having been discreet matchmaker for the Hesses and the Czarevitch, he was commissioned to play the same delicate part for the Czarevitch's daughters.

He was living now in the Rue de la Chaussée d'Antin. His love of music was still strong, and on young Mozart's visits to Paris, Grimm was his kindest and most influential patron. The next few years saw the deaths of many old friends—of Voltaire, of Diderot, of Frederick the Great, of d'Holbach, and of Madame d'Épinay. For ever trying to conciliate all men, poor little volatile, self-deceived deceiver, under Grimm's masterful influence the best qualities of her nature had come to the fore and the worst receded. She was to the last true to him as she had never been true to anyone else. Grimm adopted her granddaughter and married her to the Comte de Bueil.

So far, his own life had been singularly happy and successful. If he had loved unwisely, he had taken care that the affection should never be of that inordinate kind which is its own punishment. He had, too, one of the dearest solaces of declining life in seeing young people growing up about him. As to his career, he was not only attached to the royal house of Orleans, but he was by now Catherine's Councillor of State, Minister Plenipotentiary to the Duke of Saxe-Gotha, and Baron of the Viennese Empire. He was a rich man, with a fine collection of books, pictures, and *vertu*. He should have died before 1789.

In that year came the stunning fall of the Bastille. Of liberty, Grimm had talked easily enough, but he had also been shrewd enough to doubt its promises. He had at least nothing of the calm confidence of the fine ladies of the old *régime* who drove out from modish Paris through the Faubourg Saint-Antoine to look at the ruins of the great prison, as at a sight prepared—for their amusement. To the wary German the destruction of the Bastille spelt the ruin of France. The Revolution sped on—Vengeance rushing through the night with a drawn sword in her hand.

In 1790 came the great emigration of the nobles. Who should be suspect if not this correspondent of kings? Grimm fled to Frankfort; but in two months' time he plunged again into the whirlpool of Paris, to rescue the Comtesse de Bueil, his dear adopted grandchild, then in sore straits. He took her to Aix-la-Chapelle; but in October 1791 he returned himself to the capital, to get the Empress's letters out of France if he could. He found he had already been denounced in the committees as carrying on a correspondence with her 'little favourable to the Revolution.' His only chance of safety lay, he saw, in 'extreme circumspection.' He had that quality by nature to the full; but, none the less, stirred by a generous pity, history tells of an interview he had with the royal saint, Madame Elisabeth, in which he tried to assist both her and Marie Antoinette. He could do nothing; fate and the fatal Bourbon character were too strong for the Bourbons to be saved.

In 1792 Grimm, who had loved her long and owed her much, said farewell to Paris for ever, leaving behind him, as he said, the fruit of the wisdom of his whole life and his entire fortune, and finding himself as naked as when he came into the world. He and Madame de Bueil lodged over a chemist's shop in Düsseldorf, and even had to sleep in the Natural History Museum of that town. Grimm's whole income was Catherine's pension of two thousand roubles; her generosity indeed often added to it, and in 1796 she made him Russian Minister at Hamburg. This was one of the last acts of her life. She died, and left her friend and servant yet the poorer for her loss.

At Hamburg he had a disease of the eye which necessitated its removal. Then he retired to Gotha and lived with the Comtesse de Bueil in a house given him by the Duke of Saxe-Gotha, the munificent Duke providing furniture, linen, kitchen utensils—everything. The Countess's two young daughters acted as Grimm's secretaries. The music he had loved was still a resource to him, and he seems to have kept to the last something of his old power and mastery over others. Goethe found him, when he saw him in 1801, still an agreeable man of the world and rich in interest and experience, but unable to conceal a profound bitterness at the thought of his misfortunes. Under the Directory some of his confiscated property was restored to him. But it could hardly benefit him; he no longer lived, he only existed. He, who had been born when the Regent Orleans ruled France and the old order was at the supreme height of its magnificence and depravity, was roused from the dotage of his last days to hear the thunder of the cannon of Jena and Austerlitz, or the story of the peace concluded between Catherine's grandson, Alexander, and Napoleon Bonaparte upon the raft at Tilsit.

Grimm died on December 19, 1807, aged eighty-four.
No unpleasing contrast, this 'methodical, adroit, managing man,' with his cold uprightness and steady prudence, to a reckless, out-at-elbows Diderot, or a mad, miserable Rousseau. Thriftiness and caution are unromantic virtues and even accounted selfish; but, after all, the world would have no beggars to relieve if every man laid by for himself.

If it was the Encyclopædists' mission to teach the people to reform their kings, it was Grimm's to teach those kings to reform themselves—to be as careful and judicious as he was. He tried; but from long and close association with them he himself caught at last that disease epidemic among rulers—oblivion to unpleasant consequences and a relentless future—and never recovered from the fearful shock which opened his eyes at last.

VII: HELVÉTIUS: THE CONTRADICTION

Most of the reforming philosophers of the eighteenth century were better in word than deed.
Helvétius wrote himself down self-seeker and materialist, and in every action of his life gave his utterance the lie. Helvétius was, as Voltaire had been, a courtier—not the teacher of kings, like Grimm, but their friend and servant. Helvétius alone was at once of that body, which of all bodies the philosophers most hated, the Farmers-General—the extortionate tax-gatherers of old France—and of a practical philanthropy Voltaire himself might have envied.
He belonged to a family famous in the medical profession. His great-grandfather, a religious refugee from the Palatinate, had been a clever quack, practising in Holland. His grandfather introduced ipecacuanha to the doctors of Paris, and his father, having saved Louis XV's life in some childish complaint, was made physician to the Queen and Councillor of State. Still the family fortunes were but mediocre. Little Claude-Adrien, who was born in 1715, was at first educated at home by a mother 'full of sweetness and goodness.' Her tenderness, perhaps, was an ill preparation for the harsher, wider world of the famous school of Saint Louis-le-Grand, whither Claude-Adrian was presently sent. It was Voltaire's old school, and it was Voltaire's old schoolmaster, Père Porée, who helped the shy, sensitive, new boy with kindliness and encouragement, and first roused in him a love of letters. Grimm, who nearly always has his pen pointed with malice when he writes of Helvétius, records that poor Claude-Adrien always seemed stupid at school through being the victim of a chronic cold in the head: an unromantic affliction, which would make genius itself uninteresting. Young Helvétius was no genius, however. After leaving school he was sent to an uncle, who was a superintendent of taxes at Caen, to learn finance. There he wrote the usual boyish tragedy of promise—never to be performed—and the usual youthful verses, and was made a member of the Caen Literary Academy. The sensitive shyness soon disappeared. Young, healthy, and handsome, loving literature much and women more, an excellent dancer and fencer, clever, cool, agreeable, and much minded to get on in the world, young Helvétius comes up to Paris. At three-and-

twenty, in 1738, being the son of his father, and having the necessary financial equipment, he was made Farmer-General, a post certain to bring in two or three thousand a year, and possibly, with the requisite extortion and unscrupulousness, a good deal more.

Paris, in the years between 1738 and 1751, was certainly the most delightful and the most seductive city in the world. In the early part of that period, Madame de Tencin, the mother of d'Alembert and the sister of the Cardinal, was forming the youth of the capital in her famous *salon*. In the later period, Madame de Pompadour was revealing to it by her example the whole secret of worldly success—a clear head and a cold heart. The Court was eternally laughing, play-acting, intriguing. For the few, the world went with the liveliest lilt; and for the many—the many were dumb.

Helvétius was one of the few. Now at Madame de Tencin's, 'gathering in order that he might one day sow;' now in the *foyer* of the Comédie, where Mademoiselle Gaussin, the charming comic actress, nourished a hopeless passion for him; now at the opera, seeing for the first time Buffon, Diderot, d'Alembert, and joining hotly in the question of French or Italian music, which agitated the capital a thousand times more than national glory or shame; now at Madame de Pompadour's famous little dinners of the Entresol, or at Court, daintily distinguishing between the Queen of reality and the poor Queen *en titre*—the new young Farmer-General was Everywhere where Everybody who is Anybody goes, and Nowhere where Nobody goes. Be sure there was a fashionable shibboleth then as there is now, and be sure Helvétius prattled it and lived up to it. Grimm declared that if the word 'gallant' had not been in the French language, it would certainly have had to be invented in order to describe him.

One day, society heard of him dancing at the opera under the mask of the famous dancer, Dupré. The next, he was whispered to be the lover of a modish Countess, who had taken Atheism as other women took Jansenism, Molinism, or a craze for little dogs, and passionately imbued her lover with the exhilarating doctrine of All from Nothing to Nothing. Then he posed as the *amant-en-titre* of the Duchesse de Chaulnes. For the passions were only a pose—like the opera dancing. Helvétius was merely minded to get on in the world, and was looking about for the shortest cut to glory. He soon saw, or thought he saw, a pleasant road thereto called Verse. Voltaire, now retired to Cirey, science, and Madame du

VII: HELVÉTIUS: THE CONTRADICTION

Châtelet, had made poetry the fashion. I too will be a poet! The young Farmer-General racked his sharp brains a little, and as a result sent Voltaire some long, dismal cantos on 'Happiness.' The master replied with the kindliest criticism, and offered advice so keen and excellent that if poets were made, not born, Helvétius' verses might still live. But, after all, advice by post is always unsatisfactory. Helvétius' Farmer-Generalship made periodical tours in the provinces an agreeable necessity. On a journey through Champagne, what more natural than to stop awhile at Cirey, where Voltaire was writing 'Mahomet,' and Madame du Châtelet was the most delightful of blue-stocking hostesses? Between Arouet of five-and-forty and Claude-Adrien of five-and-twenty a warm friendship was cemented. All Voltaire's correspondence from 1738 until 1771 is studded with letters to Helvétius. The young man was his 'very dear child,' 'my rival, my poet, my philosopher.' If he took so large and liberal a view of Helvétius' talents as to declare that, as a poet, he had as much imagination as Milton, only more smoothness and regularity (!), yet he was not afraid to wrap up the pill of many a shrewd home truth in the fine sugar-plums of compliments.

But, after all, *is* poetry the easiest way to glory? Claude-Adrien, returned to Paris, walking through the Tuileries gardens one day, saw the hideous Maupertuis, the geometrician, surrounded by all the charming and pretty women, adoring him, and immediately decided to abandon verse and be a geometrician instead. But before he had taken a couple of steps in this direction, the publication of the 'Spirit of Laws' in 1748 electrified Europe, and changed his mind. To be sure, when, three years earlier, Montesquieu had brought the book up to Paris and asked the young Farmer-General's judgment on it, Helvétius had replied that it was altogether unworthy of the author of the 'Persian Letters,' and had strongly recommended him not to publish it. Well, that advice can be conveniently forgotten. Helvétius paid Montesquieu the sincerest of all flattery by resolving on the spot to be a philosopher himself.

If, between these eventful years of three-and-twenty and six-and-thirty, Helvétius had been nothing but an astute, ambitious young man-about-town, seeking the likeliest way to fame and fortune, he would have been undistinguishable from hundreds of others around him, and not worth distinguishing. But, at his worst, there was something in him which was never in that selfish crowd which thronged the galleries of

Versailles.

As tax-gatherer, it was his interest and profession to extract the uttermost farthing—and he did not do it. Nay, he pleaded in high places for the wretches it was his business to ruin. When in Bordeaux they rebelled against an iniquitous new tax on wine, he encouraged the rebellion. Though he was constantly at Court and in a position which entailed lavish personal expenditure, he pensioned Thomas, the poet, out of his own pocket; and by an annuity of a thousand écus opened the world of letters to Saurin, hereafter the dramatist. The Abbé Sabatier de Castres declared himself to have been the recipient of his delicate and generous charity. Marivaux, the novelist and playwright, who was personally very uncongenial to Helvétius, received from him a yearly sum of two thousand livres.

It was in Helvétius' house in Paris, as he afterwards told Hume, the historian, that he concealed, coming and going for 'nearly two years,' Prince Charles Edward, the Young Pretender, at a time 'when the danger was greater in harbouring him in Paris than in London' on account of the clause in the treaty of Aix-la-Chapelle of the year 1748, which stipulated that France should shelter no member of the family in her domains. Helvétius, like many another generous dupe, fell a victim to the Stuart grace and charm: 'I had all his correspondence pass through my hands; met with his partisans upon the Pont Neuf; and found at last I had incurred all this danger and trouble for the most unworthy of all mortals,' for a poor coward who 'was so frightened when he embarked on his expedition to Scotland' that he had literally to be carried on board by his attendants. (It is fair to say that Helvétius made this statement only on the testimony of a third person whose name is not given.) The sole good quality, indeed, his host ended by finding in this faint hope of Britain, the guest for whom he had risked his safety and spent his money, was that he was 'no bigot.' As this meant he had 'learnt a contempt of all religions from the philosophers in Paris,' not everyone would consider even this an advantage.

In 1740, Madame de Graffigny, famous as the gossiping visitor at Cirey with whom Voltaire and Madame du Châtelet quarrelled, had arrived in Paris, and there, in the Rue d'Enfer, near the Luxembourg, had set up her *salon*. To insure its success, Madame, who was five-and-forty, fat and unbeautiful, had with her a charming niece, Mademoiselle Anne Catherine de Ligniville, who was then one-and-twenty,

VII: HELVÉTIUS: THE CONTRADICTION

fair, handsome, intelligent. A year or two before, her aunt had adopted and so rescued her from a convent, to which the fact of the unfortunate girl having nineteen living brothers and sisters had condemned her.

In 1747, Madame de Graffigny attained celebrity by her 'Letters from a Peruvian.' Turgot did her the honour of criticising them: frequented her *salon*, which rapidly became famous, and at which, in 1750, Helvétius, still young, rich, agreeable, and unmarried, became a constant visitor. For a year, he was there perpetually. 'The sheepfold of *bel esprit*,' people called it. Helvétius liked to be thought a *bel esprit*, and it was *de rigueur* to admire the hostess's 'Peruvian' and her play 'Cénie,' which was produced in 1750. He soon came to admire something besides her writings. 'Minette,' as she nicknamed her niece, was such a woman as fashionable eighteenth-century society rarely produced—such a woman as any fashionable society rarely produces. Strong in mind and body, good, straightforward and serene, refreshingly unconventional in an age which had no god but the *convenances*, not half so clever as that accomplished old fool, her aunt, and a hundred times more sensible—such was Mademoiselle de Ligniville,

Helvétius studied her in his calm manner for a year, and at the end of it proposed to her. Then he resigned his Farmer-Generalship with its rich income; bought, to pacify his father, the post of *maître d'hotel* to Queen Marie Leczinska, and the estates of Voré and Lumigny in Burgundy, and, on June 17, 1751, married Mademoiselle de Ligniville, who was a Countess of the Holy Roman Empire, satisfactorily connected with the nobility, and had not a single franc to her *dot*.

All these actions caused something very like consternation in the world in which Helvétius lived. Give up a Farmer-Generalship! The man must be mad! 'So you are not insatiable, then, like the rest of them?' says Machault, the Controller-General. As to the estates in Burgundy, one might as well be buried alive at once! While to marry a woman who is by now certainly not a day less than two-and-thirty, has not an écu, and has a tribe of hungry brothers and sisters clinging to her, as it were, is certainly not the act of a sane person! Followed by the mingled pity and contempt of all Paris, Helvétius and his wife left immediately for Voré, and settled down to the eight happiest years of their lives.

Voré was one of those country estates which would still be called dull. In those days, before railways, with a starving

peasantry at its gates, with rare posts of the most erratic description, and with the vilest impassable roads between one country house and another, it might have been called not merely dull, but dismal. But, after all, happiness is what one is, not where one is. Perfectly content with each other, the Helvétius would have been contented in a wilderness.
Minette, says a biographer, asked nothing better than to adore her husband and perpetually to sacrifice herself to him.
If it was not in his calmer nature to adore anyone, his love for her is on the testimony of the whole eighteenth century. His married happiness 'bewildered and astonished' it. 'Those Helvétius,' said a country neighbour discontentedly, 'do not even pronounce the words, *my husband, my wife, my child*, as we others do.' 'Good husband, good father, good friend, good man,' wrote unfavourable Grimm. The easy prosperity of Helvétius' love for his wife, its freedom from storm and stress, left it, doubtless, a lighter thing than if it had been forged in the fire and beaten by the blows of affliction and reverse. It was thus with all his qualities. Kind, rather than lovable; charming, rather than great; equable, because nothing in his destiny came to move the deep waters, or because there were no deep waters to be moved: these were the keynotes to Helvétius' character.
The first child of the marriage, a daughter, was born in 1752, and the second, also a daughter, in 1754. Father and mother devoted themselves to the education of the little girls, though in their time polite society considered that parents had sufficiently obliged their children by bringing them into the world, and that further favours, such as a judicious training, were entirely superfluous.
The household was completed by two superannuated secretaries, whom Helvétius kept, very characteristically, not because he wanted them, but because he feared no one else would want them either. One of them, Baudot, had known his master from a child, and spoke to him as if he were one still. 'I have certainly not *all* the faults Baudot finds in me,' observed Helvétius tranquilly, 'but I have some of them. Who would tell me of them if I did not keep him?'
Sometimes visitors came to Voré, but for so sociable an age, not very often. Though they were always made generously welcome, they must have known they were not necessary to that *ménage*. Still, they were useful, if only to prove to these married lovers how much happier they were alone—just as the four gay winter months they spent in Paris doubled the

VII: HELVÉTIUS: THE CONTRADICTION

delights of peaceful Voré.
The day there began with work. Helvétius was now firmly minded to achieve glory by means of philosophy—fame and sport, it is said, were the only passions he had. He spent the whole morning writing and thinking. In composition he had neither the hot haste of Diderot nor the glittering inspiration of Voltaire. He wrote indeed painfully and laboriously—as the author born writes when he is weary and disinclined—as a man always writes whom nature has intended for another occupation. Sometimes one of the incompetent secretaries had to wait for hours with his pen in his hand, while his master wrestled with the refractory thought in his brain, or waited for the inspired phrase to come down from on high. His wife had not much sympathy with his philosophies. The philosophers talked so much, and as yet had done so little! But in everything else she was entirely at one with her husband.
It would be absurd to pretend that before the Revolution there were no noblemen in France who did their duty by their country estates and tenants, who looked after the poor on their lands, and, so far as they could, realised and acted up to the responsibilities of their position. There is always more goodness in the world than there appears to be, because goodness is of its very nature modest and retiring. But that the conscientious landowner was then a rare and surprising phenomenon is proved by the fact that when Helvétius and his wife began to devote themselves to acts of benevolence, everyone turned and stared at them. To-day, indeed, Helvétius might not be counted extraordinarily charitable. But it is not by modern standards he can be fairly judged. Compare him with the immense majority of the great financial magnates of his day and country, and he stands proven a philanthropist indeed.
When he first bought Voré, he had given a M. de Vasconcelles, a poor gentleman who owed the estate a large sum, a receipt for the whole, putting it into his hands saying, 'Take this paper to keep my people from bothering you;' and he further settled a handsome gift of money on him, to help him to educate his family. One of his next actions was to bring a good doctor to the place, establish him on it, and himself pay for the medical services thus rendered the peasants. Daily he and Minette visited the poor, accompanied by this doctor and a Sister of Mercy. He also set up in the place a stocking manufactory— and so, perhaps, supplied an idea to Voltaire. He encouraged and helped the farmers to farm their land; acted as unpaid

judge in their disputes; and in hard times let them off their debts. There are a dozen stories of the private individuals he helped. One day, it is a ruined Jesuit priest, who has abused his confidence and kindness. Helvétius finds one of the Jesuit's friends, and gives him fifty louis for his old enemy. 'Do not say it comes from me—he has injured me, and he would feel humiliated at receiving a gift from me.' Could delicacy go further?

Another day, when he was driving, a woodman leading a horse and cart was irritatingly slow in getting out of the way of the carriage. Helvétius lost his patience. 'All right,' said the man, 'I am a *coquin* and you are an honest man, I suppose, because I am on foot and you are in a carriage.' 'I beg your pardon,' says Helvétius, with his fine instincts instantly awake, 'you have given me an excellent lesson, for which I ought to pay;' and he gave the man a sum which, though handsome, was less generous than the apology.

When famine came to Voré, Helvétius' deep purse and wise judgment were both to the fore. Did the man accomplish less good because, though his heart was kind, it was not warm; because, though he relieved suffering, there was that in his temperament which saved him from suffering with it? If the philanthropist must have either a cool head or a hot heart, better the cool head a thousand times. He will do much less harm.

Many of Helvétius' charities were performed through his valet, whom he bade say nothing about them, even after his death. Sometimes he concealed from his wife, and she concealed from him, the good deeds of which each had been guilty.

A peasant had been imprisoned for poaching on Helvétius' grounds, and his gun confiscated. Helvétius went to him, bought back his gun, paid his fine, and had him set free, begging his silence because Minette had warned him to be severe with the man as he deserved. That warning troubled her generous heart. She too went to the culprit, gave him money to pay his fine and repurchase his gun, and vowed him to secrecy. Whether the peasant kept the secrets (as well as the price of two fines and two guns), and husband and wife confessed to each other, history does not relate.

There is, indeed, a reverse side to Helvétius' character as enlightened landowner. Carlyle, in his 'Essay on Diderot,' quotes Diderot's 'Voyage a Bourbonne,' in which the ex-Farmer-General is portrayed as a cruelly strict preserver,

VII: HELVÉTIUS: THE CONTRADICTION

living in the midst of peasants who broke his windows, plundered his garden, tore up his palings, and hated him so savagely that he dared not go out shooting save with an armed escort of four-and-twenty keepers. Diderot added that Helvétius had swept away a little village of huts which the poor people had built on the fringe of his preserves; that the good philosopher was a coward, and the unhappiest of men. But it must be remembered that Diderot did not speak from first-hand observation, but drew, and said he drew, all his information from a Madame de Nocé, a neighbour of Helvétius. Now happy, unsociable people like Helvétius and his wife are not likely to be popular in a limited country society, which would expect much from them, and get practically nothing. Saint-Lambert and Marmontel both speak of Helvétius' liberality, generosity, and unostentatious benevolence. Morellet, who was his closest intimate for many years, adds like testimony, and especially mentions his mercy to poachers. One story illustrating it has been told. Another runs that Helvétius found a man poaching under the very windows of his house, and at first naturally inclined to wrath, curbed himself: 'If you wanted game, why did you not ask me? I would have given it to you.'

Perhaps the truth of the whole matter lies in that anecdote. The keen sportsman and preserver did sometimes lose his temper and forget his compassion: his better self soon recalled it, and that rare disposition of humility and love for his fellows hastened to make amends.

In 1755, the book to which he had devoted those long, laborious mornings at Voré (by which I must certainly achieve glory, if I am to achieve it at all!) was finished at last. It was to be called 'De l'Esprit' — not to be translated 'Wit,' as Croker translated it, but something much more serious — 'On the Mind.'

It set out to prove a new theory of human action, and a new system of morality. Virtue and vice? There are no such things. Self-interest, rightly understood, is the explanation of the one, and self-interest, misunderstood, of the other. Selfishness and the passions are the sole mainsprings of our deeds. So far from character being destiny, as Novalis is to declare, destiny is in all cases character. Everybody is the creature of his environment and his education. Free Will? What free will to be an honest man has the child of thieves, brought up to thieve in a slum? Change his condition, and you change him. Leave him, and he will steal as certainly as fire burns and the waves beat on the shore. As for the vaunted superiority of the human intelligence over the brutes, 'an accident of physical organisation' can account for that. We are as the brutes, only a little better, and the difference is wholly of degree, not of kind. Put these theories, with their showy falsehood and their substratum of truth, on the library table of any clever man, and get him to do his best to prove them by sophistry and ingenuity, by trick, by subterfuge, by illustration—somehow, anyhow, so that he prove them to the hilt—and the result will be pretty well what Helvétius made it. There was scarcely a good story, or a bad one, he had heard in his early gay life in Paris that he did not bring in, by hook or by crook, to point and enliven his paradox. Madame de Graffigny told Bettinelli that nearly all the notes were the 'sweepings' of her *salon*. 'On the Mind' is entertaining or nothing—difficulties presented solely that they may be wittily demolished—easy, inaccurate, trifling; a style 'insinuating and caressing ... made for light minds, young people and women,' says Damiron; a book which fashion might skip at its toilette, and then, on the strength of remembering two or three of its dubious anecdotes, claim a complete knowledge of its *bizarre* philosophy. For it was but a *bizarrerie*—a *jeu d'esprit*—and Helvétius knew it. He was merely concerned to see how far his impossible theories could be made plausible, and wrote them to catch the public ear, and turn their author into the lion and darling of the season.

When the thing was ready he took it to Tercier, the censor, who passed it, suggesting only the omission of a few too complimentary references to free-thinking Hume. Helvétius cut them out. Malesherbes, during its printing, observed uneasily that the book contained 'some very strong things'— insolent remarks, for instance, on that dear, crusted old despotism under which we all live, and certainly a suggestion that any means to overthrow tyranny are permissible. But, all the same, in May 1758 it received its privilege. Majesty was graciously pleased to accept a copy from the author, our *maître d'hôtel*. It was already in the hands of the philosophers. And everybody began to read.

It would not have been wonderful, if the theories had had a little more *vraisemblance*, that most people, particularly people who had devoted their lives and their fortunes to others, who had laboured in poverty that other men might be free and rich, should object to see their self-denial set down as self-interest, and to be informed that the highest aspiration of their soul was really nothing but a morbid condition of the body. But, considering their manifest absurdity, it is wonderful that these assertions were taken seriously.

Madame du Defiand, indeed, might naturally say that in making self-interest the mainspring of conduct, Helvétius had revealed everybody's secret. He had so certainly discovered hers. But Turgot, whose life was to do good, had better have laughed at an absurdity than have risen up to condemn it as 'philosophy without logic, literature without taste, and morality without goodness.' A Condorcet, whose long devotion to duty was rewarded only with ruin and death, need not have troubled to loathe it. Rousseau immediately sat down to refute it: some of the most inspired pages of his 'Savoyard Vicar' still glow with the hatred with which it inspired him. Grimm wisely only pooh-poohed it. Voltaire grumbled that his pupil had promised a book on the Mind, and presented a treatise on Matter; that he had 'put friendship among the bad passions,' and, much worse than all, has actually compared me—me—to two such feeble, second-rate luminaries as Crébillon and Fontenelle! No wonder that he found the title, 'De l'Esprit,' equivocal, the matter unmethodical, all the new things false and all the old ones truisms.

For a very short time, however, approved or disapproved, taken as folly or mistaken for reason, the book went its way gaily. It bade fair to become what Helvétius had meant it to be —the success of a season. But for the besotted stupidity of the Government, it never would have been anything else.

One unlucky day the Dauphin, who was more virtuous than wise, came out of his room with a copy in his hand and fury in his face. 'I am going to show the Queen the sort of thing her *maître d'hôtel* prints.

On August 10, 1758, the privilege for its publication was revoked. Tercier was deprived of his office. 'On the Mind' was furiously attacked in the religious papers. The *avocat général*, Fleury, pronounced it 'an abridgment of the Encyclopædia.' The Archbishop of Paris declared it struck at the roots of Christianity. At Court, Helvétius was all at once 'regarded as a child of perdition, and the Queen pitied his mother as if she had produced Anti-Christ.' Rome banned the accursed thing. On January 31, 1759, the Pope attacked it with his own hand in a letter. On February 6 the Parliament of Paris condemned it. On February 10 it was publicly burned by the hangman, with Voltaire's 'Natural Law.' On April 9 the Sorbonne censured it, and declared it to contain 'the essence of the poisons' of all modern literature.

Helvétius, from being the happiest of easygoing, benevolent philosophers, found himself, as it were in a second, in a position of great danger, and what Collé in his Journal called 'cruel pain.' His friends hotly urged upon him a retractation to soften the certain punishment awaiting him. His mother begged it from him with tears. Only Minette, a sterner and a braver soul, refused, though 'a great personage' besought her, to add her own entreaties to that end.

Still, it had to be done. Something of a coward this Helvétius, as Collé suggested now, as Diderot had suggested before? The rich and easy life he had led does not breed courage certainly. But, after all, Helvétius only did what Voltaire and many a better man declared it was essential to do in that day. He produced a 'Letter from the Reverend Father ... Jesuit,' in which he stated that he had written in perfect innocence and simplicity, and (this was undoubtedly true) that he had not had the slightest idea of the effect his book would create. He added, in the stiff phraseology of the time, words to the effect that he was an exceedingly religious man and very sorry indeed. The *amende* was so far accepted that the Parliament simply condemned him to give up his stewardship, and exiled him for two years to Voré.

What the book could never have done for itself, or for its author, persecution did for them both. 'On the Mind' became not the success of a season, but one of the most famous books of the century. The men who had hated it, and had not particularly loved Helvétius, flocked round him now. Voltaire forgave him all injuries, intentional or unintentional. 'What a fuss about an omelette!' he had exclaimed when he heard of the burning. How abominably unjust to persecute a man for such an airy trifle as that! 'I disapprove of what you say, but I will defend to the death your right to say it,' was his attitude now. But he soon came, as a Voltaire would come, to swearing that there was no more materialism in 'On the Mind' than in Locke, and a thousand more daring things in 'The Spirit of Laws.' Turgot and Condorcet forgave the philosophy, in their pity for the philosopher. D'Alembert made common cause with the man with whom he had nothing else in common. Rousseau instantly stopped writing his refutation. Diderot roundly swore 'On the Mind' was one of the great books of the age. Though Rome had censured it, cardinals wrote to condole with its author on the treatment it had received. It was translated into almost all European languages. Presently, England published an edition of her own. And Helvétius, when that two years' exile—a punishment surely only in name?—was over, returning to Paris, found himself the most distinguished man in the capital.

In their fine hotel in the Rue Sainte-Anne (Rue Helvétius, the municipality of 1792 rechristened it, and Rue Saint-Helvétius, the *cochers* of Paris!) he and his wife received the flower of French society. Turgot introduced to them Morellet, who soon became a daily visitor, rode with them in the Bois, and stayed with them in the country. To their Tuesday dinners at two o'clock came Condorcet, d'Alembert, Diderot, d'Holbach, Galiani, Marmontel, Saint-Lambert, Raynal, Gibbon, and Hume—'the States-General of the human mind,' says Garat. Only time-serving Buffon, in order not to offend the Court, gave up visiting at the house. If Galiani found the religious, or irreligious, views of the *salon* too free, Madame his hostess shared his opinion, and would often purposely disturb a too daring conversation by drawing aside one of the coterie to talk with her *à part*. Helvétius himself was still, as he had ever been, listener rather than talker; or talker chiefly when he laid before his friends, with a *naïveté* and simplicity wholly at variance with the sophistry and artificiality of his writing, the difficulties he had encountered in it that morning, or some theories which it had suggested.

Sometimes, directly dinner was over, he slipped out to the opera, and left his wife to do the honours alone. When they were not entertaining themselves, they rarely went out, unless it were on Fridays to Madame Necker's. 'Jealous of his wife,' said acid Grimm, accounting for this unsociability, 'Happy with her,' is perhaps a truer solution.

But if their own *entourage* was thus satisfactory, the Court was still bitterly hostile. Though Helvétius, of course, knew very well that that hostility had been the advertisement to which his book owed everything, still, its injustice rankled.

Admiring England invited him to her shores; and on March 10, 1764, he landed there, accompanied by his two daughters, Elizabeth and Genevieve, who, being only ten and twelve years respectively, were certainly rather young for their father to be seeking husbands for them among 'the immaculate members of our august and incorruptible senate,' as Horace Walpole declared that he was.

All the great people, including King George the Third, received the persecuted philosopher with *empressement*.

'Savants and politicians' flocked to be introduced to him. Gibbon found him 'a sensible man, an agreeable companion, and the worthiest creature in the world.' Hume (remembering the compliments it contained and the many more it would have contained but for that wretched censor) naturally thought 'On the Mind' the most pleasing of writings, and had even entered into an agreement with its author to translate it into English, if he, on his part, would translate Hume's philosophical works into French. (This bargain was never concluded.) Warburton, indeed, declined to meet this French 'rogue and atheist' at dinner. But Helvétius, as a whole, had every reason to like Englishmen, and he came back to France, Diderot told Mademoiselle Volland, as madly attached to England as d'Holbach was the reverse. 'This poor Helvétius,' says Diderot, to excuse him, 'saw only in England the persecutions his book had brought him in France.' There may certainly be truth in that.

A year later, in 1765, he went to stay with Frederick the Great. That astute monarch had not at all approved of 'On the Mind.' 'If I wanted to punish a province, I would give it to philosophers to govern,' said he. But he found Helvétius, as all the world found him, a thousand times better than his book, and observed very justly that in writing he had much better have consulted his heart than his head.

But that was what Helvétius could never do.

When he got back to Voré, to Minette and the little daughters (he had not found any spotless and disinterested members of parliament to marry them and enjoy their fortunes of fifty thousand pounds apiece), he settled down to literature again and wrote, with seven years' severe and unremitting labour, 'On Man, his Intellectual Faculties, and his Education,' which was a sort of defence of 'On the Mind' and an answer to the criticisms both friends and foes had brought against that work. If he had been persistently lively on 'Mind,' he was persistently dull on 'Man.' When it was published, after his death, only a few friends who had loved its author defended it. Mademoiselle de Lespinasse voiced a very general opinion when she declared herself 'staggered' at its preposterous length; and Grimm (of course) declared that, for his part, he would rather have ten lines of the dear little Abbé Galiani than ten volumes such as that.

Meanwhile, it had given Helvétius the best solace chagrins and declining life can have—a regular occupation. He was not old, and he was framed, says Guillois, to be a centenarian. But

VII: HELVÉTIUS: THE CONTRADICTION

at that epoch men spent their health and strength with such fearful prodigality in their youth, that they rarely lived beyond what is now called middle age. Helvétius was not more than five-and-fifty when he became conscious of failing powers. Sport, which had been the delight of his life, lost its zest. The bankrupt condition of his country, her light-hearted descent to ruin, lay heavily now on a soul framed by nature to take the world serenely and to see the future fair. He was occupied, it is true, to the end in those works of benevolence and kindness which pay an almost certain interest in happiness to him who invests in them. Then, too, to the last, there was his wife, who might have loved a better man than he, but who—love, fortunately for most people, not being given entirely to worth—spent on him the fidelity and devotion of her life.
On December 26, 1771, Helvétius died. He was buried in the Church of Saint-Roch, in Paris.
Minette, a very rich widow, bought a house in Auteuil, where, visited by Turgot, Condorcet, Benjamin Franklin, Morellet, and the famous young doctor, Cabanis, she lived 'to love those her husband had loved, and to do good to those he had benefited.' Franklin, it is said, would fain have married her. And Turgot—who knows? Elizabeth and Genevieve, enormously rich heiresses, were married on the same day, a year after their father's death, each to a Count.
In 1772, 'On Man' was published, with the reception which has been recorded. That early poem, 'Happiness,' also now publicly appeared for the first time, with a prose preface by Saint-Lambert—the prose, said Galiani, being much better than the verse.
To Helvétius' works, or rather to his work, for 'On the Mind' is the only one that counts, is now generally meted the judgment which should have been meted to it when it appeared. Catch thistledown, imprison it, examine it beneath a microscope, and a hundred learned botanists will soon be confabulating and fighting over it. Put it in the free air and sunshine—and, lo! it is gone. 'On the Mind' was but thistledown, and the winds have blown it away.
But the man who wrote it deserves recollection because, though he wrote it, he and Turgot alone among their compeers realised in practice that the best way to do good to mankind is to do good to individual man, here and to-day, and that the surest means to relieve the sorrows of the world is to help the one poor Lazarus lying, full of sores, at the gate.

VIII: TURGOT: THE STATESMAN

Among Voltaire's friends Turgot and Condorcet at least were not merely great, but also good men. Even Condorcet, though himself of virtuous and noble life, had not that high standard of living, that sterner modern code of purity and uprightness, which were remarkably Turgot's.

But Turgot was something more even than the best man of his party. He was the best worker. While Voltaire clamoured and wept for humanity, while d'Alembert thought, Grimm wrote, Diderot talked, and Condorcet dreamed and died, Turgot laboured. Broad and bold in aim, he was yet content to do what he could. Of him it might never be said 'L'amour du mieux t'aura interdit du bien.' To do one's best here and now, with the wretched tools one has to hand, in the teeth of indolence, obstinacy, and the spirit of routine, to compromise where one cannot overcome, and instead of sitting picturing some golden future, to do at once the little one can—that was this statesman's policy.

It was so far successful, that all men now allow that if any human power could have stemmed the avalanche of the French Revolution, it would have been the reforms of Turgot. His father was the Provost of Merchants in Paris, and has earned the gratitude of Parisians by enlarging the Quai de l'Horloge and joining it by a bridge to the opposite bank of the Seine, and by erecting the fountain in the Rue de Grenelle de St. Germain.

Anne Robert Jacques was his third son, and a timid, shy little creature. His mother, who, *en vraie Parisienne*, thought everything of appearance and manners, worried him on the subject of his clumsiness and stupidity, which naturally made the child self-conscious and increased the faults fourfold. When visitors arrived to flatter Madame by admiring her children, Anne Robert hid under the sofa or the table; and when he was removed from his retreat, could produce no company manners at all. No wonder the mother never even suspected the strong intellect and the wonderful character that so much awkwardness concealed.

Anne Robert's birth was contemporaneous with Voltaire's visit to England, and took place on May 10, 1727. The child had already two brothers. The eldest was bound, after the

foolish custom of the day, to follow his father's profession; the second brother must go into the army; and for Anne Robert there was nothing left but the Church.
He followed Voltaire and Helvétius at the school of Louis-le-Grand, and when sufficiently advanced, moved on to the College of Plessis. As a schoolboy his pocket-money disappeared with the usual rapidity, but not in the usual way. This shy little student gave it to his poorer companions, to buy books. From the time he was sixteen—that is in 1743—until 1750, he was a divinity student. At Saint-Sulpice, whither he went in 1748 on leaving Plessis, he took his degree as a Theological Bachelor, and from there entered the Sorbonne. The Sorbonne, which was swept away by the Revolution, was a very ancient Theological College and in some respects not unlike an English university. Young Turgot found there Morellet and Loménie de Brienne, besides a certain Abbé de Cicé, to whom in 1749 he addressed one of the first of his writings, a 'Letter on Paper Money.'
In 1749, Turgot was made Prior of the Sorbonne, in which *rôle* he had to deliver two Latin lectures, choosing for his themes, 'The Advantages of Christianity,' and 'The Advance of the Mind of Man.' All the time he was reading, thinking, observing on his own account, studying especially Locke, Bayle, Clarke, and Voltaire. A priest he soon knew he could not be. To be sure, the fact that his friend Loménie de Brienne is a sceptic will not prevent him becoming a cardinal and Archbishop of Toulouse; he would have been Archbishop of Paris had his Majesty not been so painfully particular as to demand that the Primate of the capital should at least believe in a God. But Turgot was of other metal and was not minded to live a lie. All his friends begged him to keep to the lucrative career assigned him, surely, by Providence! 'You will be a bishop,' says Cicé comfortably, 'and then you can be a statesman at your leisure.'
The argument was very seductive; but this student was in every respect unlike other students, with a character breathing a higher and finer air than theirs. Morellet records, not without the suspicion of a sneer, that from their coarse boyish jokes he shrank as one shrinks from a blow. Even Condorcet, himself so pure in life, laughed at people wasting time in quenching the desires of the flesh; but Turgot vindicated purity as well as practised it, and reached a level of principle, as of conduct, which in the eighteenth century was unfortunately almost unique.

His father, wiser than most parents in like circumstances, countenanced his objections to the priesthood. He had already studied law, as well as theology. In 1750 he left the Sorbonne, and Loménie gave a farewell dinner in his rooms, with Turgot and Morellet of the party, and the light-hearted guests planned a game of tennis behind the church of the Sorbonne for the year 1800.

The year 1800! Before then the Sorbonne itself had perished with Church, monarchy, and nobility; shallow Brienne, having done mighty mischief, had poisoned himself in the château his ill-earned wealth had been gained to restore; Morellet was writing revolutionary pamphlets; and Turgot was dead.

In 1752, two years after he left the Sorbonne, Anne Robert obtained the legal post of Deputy Counsellor of the Procurator-General, and a year later was made Master of Requests.

One must picture him at this time as a tall, broad-shouldered, rather handsome man, with that old boyish constraint in his manner, and that strict high-mindedness which his own generation could not be expected to find attractive. Add to these qualities that he was not in the least carried away by dreams and visions, as were nearly all his friends, that even then he saw the world as it was, and meant to do with it what he could—that, though in lofty aim he may have been an idealist, he never fell into the idealist's fault of believing that, because there is everything to do, he must do everything, or nothing. Just, reasonable, practical—what a wholesome contrast to your visionary Rousseaus, ay, and to your impulsive Voltaires! He was not a brilliant person, this; it is said that he was slow in everything he undertook. Nor had he given over the vigour of his youth and the strength of his understanding to any one party. He was studying them all. He was about three or four and twenty when he first began to go into the intellectual society of Paris—when Montesquieu, d'Alembert, Galiani, Helvétius, found the stiffness of manner more than redeemed by the wealth of the mind. Presently he was introduced to Madame de Graffigny, and complimented her by writing a long review of her 'Letters from a Peruvian,' which, as giving his own views on education, on marriage, and on the fashionable avoidance of parenthood, retains all its interest. It is strange to hear a pre-Revolutionary Frenchman urging love-marriages—'Because we are sometimes deceived, it is concluded we ought never to choose'—and strange also that, out of all the great reformers with whom his name is

associated, Turgot alone perceived the fearful havoc which
neglect of family duties makes in the well-being of the State.
He was presented to Madame de Graffigny by her niece,
Mademoiselle de Ligniville. The bright and charming Minette
naturally did not find it at all difficult to draw Anne Robert of
five-and-twenty from the intellectual society of her aunt's
salon to a game of battledore and shuttlecock *à deux*. Morellet,
watching the pair, professed himself pained and astonished
that their friendship did not end as nearly all such friendships
do and should.

Most ol Turgot's biographers have sought the reason why
Mademoiselle de Ligniville became Madame Helvétius and
not Madame Turgot—and have not found it. As for Turgot, he
said nothing. It remains idle to speculate whether he
conceived for her a passion, which his *gaucherie* and shyness,
perhaps, prevented her from returning; or whether he had
already devoted his life to his public duty, and thought that
private happiness would be deterrent and not spur to his
work for the race. An unhappy or an unrequited affection is
one of the finest incentives to labour and success one can have.
It may be that Turgot had it. The only certain facts are that
Minette married Helvétius, and that Turgot remained her life-
long friend.

In 1754 he made the acquaintance of Quesnay and of de
Gournay, the political economists, who influenced not a little
his life and thought. He soon began writing articles for the
Encyclopædia, though he never joined in that battle-cry of the
Encyclopædists, *Écrasez l'infâme*, and was wholly without
sympathy for the atheism of d'Holbach and the materialism of
Helvétius. Turgot, indeed, may be said to have been, in the
broadest acceptation of the term, a Christian; or rather he
would be called, and call himself, a Christian to-day. But his
Christianity was not of Rome nor yet of Protestantism, but
that in whose honest doubt there lives more faith than in half
the creeds. He certainly gave little expression to it. It was the
religion of the wise man—which he never tells.

When he was on a geologising tour in Switzerland, in 1760, he
saw the great Pontiff of the Church of Antichrist at Délices.
That generous old person was warm in delight and
admiration for his guest. D'Alembert had introduced him, and
d'Alembert's friends must always be welcome. And then
Turgot's article on 'Existence' in the Encyclopædia had made
even more impression on this impressionable Voltaire than on
the world of letters in general. He took this young disciple to

his heart at once. Well, then, if he is not precisely a disciple, he is at least a most 'lovable philosopher,' and 'much fitter to instruct me than I am to instruct him!' It was Voltaire who was dazzled by the young man's splendid possibilities, not the young man who was dazzled by Voltaire's matchless fame and daring genius. Turgot was never dazzled; it was his greatness, if it was also his misfortune, to see men and the world exactly as they are.

In 1761 he was made Intendant of Limoges. It was the great opportunity; he had wanted practical work—not to think, to write, or to dream. Voltaire wrote of him afterwards as one 'qui ne chercha le vrai que pour faire le bien.' He wanted to Do; and here was everything to be done.

The picture of provincial France before the Revolution has been painted often, but the subject is one of which the painter can never tire and to which he can never do justice.

The Limoges which Turgot found was one of the most beautiful districts of France—and one of the most wretched. Here, on the one side, rose the châteaux of the great absentee noblemen, who, always at Court, left behind them middlemen to wring from the poor innumerable dues, with which my lord, forsooth, must pay his debts of honour and make a fine figure at Versailles. The few nobles who did live on their country estates expected their new young Intendant to be an agreeable social light, as his predecessors had been, who would keep, for the *élite* of the neighbourhood, an open house where one would naturally find good wine, rich fare, and delightful, doubtful company.

On the other hand were the clergy—often ignorant, but generally cunning enough to play on the deeper ignorance of their flock by threats of the Hereafter, and to keep from them that knowledge which is the death-blow of superstition.

Then there were the poor. Picture a peasantry whose homes were windowless, one-roomed huts of peat or clay; who subsisted, in times of plenty, on roots, chestnuts, and a little black bread; who had neither schools nor hospitals, teachers nor doctors; who were the constant prey of pestilence and famine; whose bodies were the possession of their lords, and whose dim souls were the perquisites of the priests. Consider that these people were not allowed to fence such miserable pieces of land as they might possess, lest they should interfere with my lord's hunting; nor to manure their wretched crops, lest they should spoil the flavour of his game; nor to weed them, lest they should disturb his partridges. Consider that, if such land could have borne any fruit, a special permission was required to allow its owners to build a shed to store it in. Consider that their villages, in which they herded like beasts, were separated from other villages by roads so vile that they would have rendered commerce difficult, if legal trammels had not made it impossible. Consider that these people had been scourged for generations by hundreds of unjust and senseless laws, made by and for the benefit of their oppressors, and that they were now the victims of taxes whose very name has become an indictment, and whose description is a justification of the French Revolution.

On the one flank they were whipped by the *taille*—the tax on the income and property of the poor, which absorbed one-half of the net products of their lands—and on the other by the *corvée*, which compelled them to give yearly twelve or fifteen days' unpaid labour on the roads and the use of a horse and cart, if they had them. The *milice* demanded from each parish its quota of soldiers (the rich being exempt as usual), and compelled the parishes to lodge passing detachments of military and to lend cattle to draw the military equipages. The *gabelle*, or tax on salt, forced each poor man to buy seven pounds of salt per annum—whether, as in one province, it was a halfpenny a pound, or, as in another, it was sixpence—and let the noble, the priest, and the Government official go free. Toll-gates were so numerous in the country that it is said fish brought from Harfleur to Paris paid eleven times its value on the journey. Wine was taxed; corn was taxed.

But this was not all. If these taxes were cruelly unjust, they were settled and regular. Irregular taxes could be levied at any moment at the caprice of the despot at Versailles, who no more realised the condition of his peasantry than an ordinary Briton realises the condition of a tribe of Hottentots. One, called with an exquisite irony the Tax of the Joyful Accession, had been raised when Louis the Tifteenth reached the throne of France—to topple it down the abyss. Another was the *vingtième*, or tax on the twentieth part of a franc, which could be doubled or trebled at the pleasure of the Government.

Apart altogether from the taxes, the peasantry were subject to tithes exacted by the Church, itself exempt from all taxation, to large fees for christening and marrying, for getting out of the misery of this world and avoiding worse misery in the next.

The clergy were on the spot to exact these dues, just as the middleman was on the spot to exact the dues for the nobles.

VIII: TURGOT: THE STATESMAN

Some of these dues and seigneurial rights are so shameful and disgusting that their very terms are unrepeatable. Even that vile age permitted many of them to lapse and become a dead letter; but the number, and the full measure of the iniquity of those that were insisted on, has never been counted, and will never be known until the Day of Judgment.

What effect would hundreds of years of such oppression have on the character of the oppressed? Hopeless, filthy, degraded, superstitious with the craven superstition which made them the easy prey of their unscrupulous clergy and left them wholly sensual and stupid; as animals, without the animals' instinctive joy of life and fearlessness of the morrow; with no ambitions for themselves or the children who turned to curse them for having brought them into such a world; with no time to dream or love, no time for the tenderness which makes life, life indeed — they toiled for a few cruel years because they feared to die, and died because they feared to live. Such were the people Turgot was sent to redeem.

What wonder that many men gave up such a task in despair; that many even good men found it easier to prophesy a Golden Age in luxurious Paris than to fight hand to hand against the awful odds of such an awful reality? Turgot was thirty-four when he went to Limoges, and forty-seven when he left it. He spent there the most vigorous years of his life; if he did not do there his most famous work, he did his noblest. He began at once. It was nothing to him that his own caste shot out the lip and scorned him. Cold and awkward in manner, regular and austere in habit, and as pure as a good woman, of course they hated him. But it was much to him that the clergy who ruled the people were also his foes, that that very people themselves were so dull and hopeless, that they too suspected his motives and concluded that because for them every change had always been for the worse, every change always would be. Slowly, gradually, he gained the favour of the priest and the love of the flock. He could not turn their hell into heaven: he could not make earth at all what Condorcet, uplifted in noble vision, would dream it yet might be. But he could do something.

In 1765, he procured for Limoges an edict restoring free trade in grain in that province. Versailles, wholly abandoned to its amusements, did not in the least care whether edicts were granted or whether they were revoked. Turgot did care. He perceived that the Court was not minded to be plagued with his reforms; and he plagued it till it gave him what he wanted

—to go away.
Then he turned to the other taxes. The existence of a privileged class which pays nothing and devours much by its shameful exactions, is itself a monstrous thing. *Taille* is the crowning iniquity; but it will take a Reign of Terror to kill it. In the meantime Turgot, in the teeth of the besotted ignorance and opposition of the wretched beings he was trying to help, could and did see that it was fairly administered.
In place of the personal service demanded by the *corvée*, he substituted a money-tax; which was better for the taxed and better also for the roads.
With regard to the *milice*, he proposed wide changes. But since the Government would not rouse itself to act on the proposals, he took advantage of its self-indulgent indifference and permitted evasions of the law; when an unlucky creature drew a black ticket in the conscription in Limoges, the new Intendant permitted him to find a substitute or to pay a fee. He also built barracks, which removed the necessity for quartering the soldiers on the poor.
The fearful trammels which 'crippled trade and industry and doomed labour to sterility,' he in part removed. He made new roads; he became President of the first Agricultural Society in the district; he founded a veterinary college. In the teeth of strong opposition he promoted the cultivation of the potato; and by having it served daily at his own table proved to the ignorance of the peasants that it was at least safe for human food. He also introduced the growth of clover, and entirely suppressed a worrying little tax on cattle. He first brought to Limoges a properly qualified midwife, who taught her business to other women. This was the beginning of the Hospice de la Maternité. During Turgot's Intendancy the china clay, of which the famous Limoges pottery was afterwards made, was discovered.
Besides these public acts, he was engaged in hundreds of small individual charities. Among others, he educated at his own expense a youth whose father had been entirely ruined by taxation and famine. The youth was Vergniaud, afterwards the stirring orator of the Revolution.
In his home-life Turgot remained most frugal and laborious, treating his servants with a benevolence then accounted contemptible, and working out his quiet schemes with an infinite patience and thoroughness. When he was offered the richer Intendancy of Lyons, he would not take it. Here, as he said of himself, though he was 'the compulsory instrument of

great evil,' he was doing a little good. Only a little, it might be. But if every man did the little he could—what a different world!

In 1765, he paid a visit to Paris, and in the Galas case, made famous by Voltaire, spoke on the side of tolerance with a vehemence unusual to him. Morellet, d'Alembert, and Mademoiselle de Lespinasse were still his friends. Condorcet was in his closest intimacy, and destined hereafter to write his Life—'one of the wisest and noblest of lives,' says John Stuart Mill, 'delineated by one of the noblest and wisest of men.'

In Paris, he met Adam Smith, the political economist. As a result of their acquaintance Turgot produced in the next year his 'Reflections on the Reformation and Distribution of Wealth,' fertile in conception, arid in style, and anticipating many of the ideas familiar to English readers through Adam Smith's 'Wealth of Nations.'

But the insistent claims of Limoges on his time and pity narrowed his hours for study, even for the study that would serve it well. In 1767 he cleared the province of wolves, by a system analogous to that by which Edgar rid Wales of the same pest.

Then, in 1770, Limoges and its Intendant began their fight with want. When Turgot came to the province, the wretched place was a million francs in arrears for its taxes. Some he had certainly lessened. The work he had started was just beginning to bear its first little harvest of good, when there came the withering blast of the two years' famine. Its horrors were unthinkable. Turgot wrote to Terrai, the Controller-General, that it was impossible to extort the taxes and the arrears without ruin—*ay, and with ruin*—to the taxed. The people could not only not pay what was demanded of them, but they had nothing to sell for the barren necessities of their own existence. God knows they had learnt by long and bitter practice to subsist on little enough! But now they must surely sit down and die.

Strong and calm, Turgot rose up again. From the Parliament at Bordeaux he obtained permission to levy a tax on the rich in aid of the sufferers. He himself opened workshops in which he gave work, and paid for it, not in coin, which would certainly be spent at the nearest cabaret, but in leather tickets which could be exchanged for food at the cheap provision shops, also of his own institution.

Far beyond his age in every practical scheme for the benefit of mankind, he was beyond our own age in that he clearly perceived that the free soup-kitchen, and all the sentimental philanthropy which gives money in lieu of work, instead of paying money for work, must be demoralising, and in the long run create more misery than it relieves. 'Such distributions,' said he, 'have the effect of accustoming the people to mendicity.' Even through a famine he sent to prison every beggar he could lay hands on. Then, again far beyond his age, he induced the ladies of the district to teach the poor girls needlework; and so to give them 'the best and most useful kinds of alms—the means to earn.' The fight was long and hard. But it had its reward. The people came to love him who had helped them to help themselves; who had given them, not the bitter bread and scornful dole of charity, but the power to earn a livelihood and their first taste of self-respect. On May 10, 1774, Louis the Sixteenth succeeded to the throne of sixty-six kings; and on July 20, Turgot was made Minister of Marine and thus called to wider and fuller work. The Limogian peasants clung about his knees with tears, and the Limogian nobles rejoiced openly at his departure. The one leave-taking was as great a compliment as the other.

The merits of this 'virtuous philosophic Turgot, with a whole reformed France in his head,' had not been in the least the reason of his promotion. But schoolfellow Cicé had whispered pleasant things of him to Madame Maurepas, the wife of the Minister; and Madame had settled the matter with her husband, who was a lively shrewd old man of seventy-four, not inconvenienced by any idea of duty, and with a very strong sense of humour.

Turgot was Minister of Marine for just five weeks; but in that time he had eighteen months' arrears of wages paid to a gang of workmen at Brest, and made many plans for the improvement of the colonies, which more than twenty years ago, at the Sorbonne, he had significantly compared to 'fruits which cling to the parent tree, only until they are ripe.' On August 24, 1774, he was made Controller-General of Finances in the place of Terrai.

It sounded a fine position, but was it? Limoges represented all France in little. A ruined Treasury, a starving people, in high places corruption and exaction, and in low places misery such as has rarely been seen since the world began.

Terrai, profligate and dissolute—'What does he want with a muff?' said witty Mademoiselle Arnould when he had appeared with one in winter; 'his hands are always in our pockets'—had left to his successor, debt, bankruptcy, chaos.

VIII: TURGOT: THE STATESMAN

The King was not quite twenty, weak with the amiable weakness which is often more disastrous in a ruler than vice. The Queen was nineteen, careless and gay, loving pleasure and her own way, and meaning to have both in spite of all the controllers in the world. Maurepas, being undisturbed by principles, would readily abandon his protégé if he perceived for himself the least danger in that patronage. Voltaire, indeed, wrote that he saw in Turgot's appointment a new heaven and a new earth, and the enlightened among the people dreamt that the Millennium had come, but Voltaire was but a voice crying in the wilderness, and in the councils of State the people had neither lot nor part.

Once again Turgot, realising to the full the difficulties, the impossibilities even, of his position, resolved to do what he could. Within a few hours of his appointment he wrote a long letter to the King, urging the absolute necessity of economy in every department, denouncing bribes, privileges, exemptions, and pleading—daring to plead—equality in the imposition of taxes. No bankruptcy, no increase of taxation, no loans—this was to be the motto of his Controllership. 'I feel all the perils to which I expose myself,' he wrote. He was not even religious in the sense—— what a sense!—that officials were expected to be religious. 'You have given me a Controller who never goes to Mass,' grumbled Louis to Maurepas. 'Sire,' answered the Minister, very happily, 'Terrai always went.'

The new Controllership was still a nine days' wonder when Turgot restored throughout France what he had restored in Limoges—free trade in grain. In 1770 he had written on the subject some famous 'Letters' in answer to Terrai's revocation of the edict and the witty 'Dialogues' of Galiani which supported that revocation. Then, bolder still, he suppressed an abominable piece of official jobbery, the *Pot de Vin,* or bribe of 100,000 crowns which the Farmers-General had always presented to the Controller when he signed a new edict. If the Farmers turned away sulkily, angry with a generosity they were by no means prepared to imitate, from the country came a long burst of passionate applause.

'It is only M. Turgot and I who love the people,' said the King. Well, this poor Louis did love them, but his was not the love that could stand firm by the man sent to save them.

'Everything for the people, nothing by them,' was Turgot's motto, and, perhaps, his mistake. The King was to be the lever to raise his kingdom; and the weak tool broke in the Minister's hand.

The first disaster of Turgot's Controllership was the disaster that spoiled his Intendancy. In 1774-5 scarcity of bread made many distrust his edict restoring to them free trade in grain. With his firm hand over Louis's shaking one he suppressed the bread riots of that winter, as it was never given to a Bourbon to suppress anything. But he would not in justice suppress, though he might have suppressed, Necker's adverse pamphlet on the question, called 'The Legislation and Commerce of Grain;' though half the Encyclopædists, and many of Turgot's personal friends, were led thereby to adopt the opinions of the solid Genevan banker.

In the January of 1775, Turgot presented his Budget. The deficit left by Terrai was enormous. Let us pay then, said Turgot's sound common-sense, the legitimate contracts of Government, not by your dear old remedy, taxation, for the ruined country can yield no more, but by limiting the expenses of that Government and of the Court. Officials and courtiers alike took as a judgment from Heaven the fact, that very shortly after this monstrous proposal, the audacious proposer was sharply attacked by the gout.

Turgot's Controllership lasted in all twenty months, and for seven of them he was very ill. When he was blamed once for overworking himself and trying to force everybody's hand, 'Why, do you not know,' he answered simply, 'in my family we die of gout at fifty?' His present illness kept him in his room many weeks, but did not prevent him from dictating an enormous correspondence, and trying urgently to persuade his master to begin his economical reforms by having his coming coronation ceremonies performed cheaply at Paris, instead of expensively at Rheims; and to make good his professions of tolerance by omitting from the service the oath binding him to extirpate heretics. Of course Louis was too weak for these drastic measures; he characteristically contented himself by mumbling the oath, and the senseless expenses of the coronation were as large as ever.

But Turgot, undaunted, went on working. In January 1776 he presented to the King what have been justly called the Six Fatal Edicts—the first for the suppression of *corvée*, four for the suppression of the offices interfering with the provisioning of Paris, and the sixth for the suppression of *jurandes* or the government of privileged corporations. The first and sixth were the real cause of battle, and embodied one of the great aims of Turgot's administration—to make the nobility and clergy contribute to the taxes.

VIII: TURGOT: THE STATESMAN

A shrill outcry of indignation rang through Versailles. Make us pay! *Us!* The Court had always scorned Turgot with his shy, quiet manner, his gentle aloofness, and the reflection cast, in the most odious taste, by the purity of his life on its own manner of living. But now it hated him. Tax *us!* Curtail *our* extravagances! Reduce *our* expenditure! What next? He has already abolished a number of our very best sinecures and lessened the salaries attached to several enticing little offices where we were enormously paid for doing nothing gracefully! He has given posts to persons fitted for them instead of to our noble and incompetent relations! If one of *us* (even when one of us is the Duc d'Orléans himself) wants to do something—well—illegal, he will not allow it! As though the makers of law could not be its breakers if they chose! And Versailles rustled indignantly in its unpaid-for silks, whispered, murmured, connived at the fall of this quiet, strong person who had not a thought in common with them—nor a thought of himself.
But he had a more dangerous enemy than the Court—the Queen. Quick-witted, wilful, impetuous, with a husband whose slow, hesitating intellect she must needs despise, clever enough to love to meddle with great things, but not wise enough to meddle well—Marie Antoinette took her first deep step down the stairway of ruin when she chose to be Turgot's enemy instead of Turgot's friend. Could he have saved her too, if she would have let him, as, but for her, men thought he might have saved France? God knows. Marie Antoinette wanted to be amused, and her particular amusement, gambling, was very expensive; she was infinitely good-natured and impetuously in love at the moment with Madame de Lamballe, and wanted for her the revival of the old post of Superintendent of the Household, with its enormous emoluments. And at her side stood Turgot, saying, 'No.' Maurepas had long since deserted him. It was much easier, and safer for one's own interest, to give the Queen what she wanted and have done with it. As for Louis, he was, as usual, weak with the weakness that brought him to the guillotine and ended the French monarchy.
Turgot so far controlled him that the six Edicts were registered by the unwilling Parliament of Paris. Then Monsieur, afterwards Louis the Eighteenth, expressed in a pamphlet of very feeble wit the feelings of the upper classes against this terrible reformer. That paltry skit had already turned the King against his Minister, when Maurepas showed him a sharp financial criticism on Turgot's calculations as Controller-

General, and some forged letters purporting to come from Turgot and containing expressions offensive to the Royal Family. Not man enough to take them to Turgot and demand explanation, the wretched King went on distrusting him and giving him feeble hints to resign.
But until there was a better man to occupy his place, Turgot would take no hints. For the sake of France he would push those Edicts through, and gain his principles before he lost his power.
Then another friend failed him. Malesherbes, the brave old hero, who was hereafter to defend and to die for his King, but who, as Condorcet said, found on every subject 'many fors and againsts but never one to make him decide,' resigned his post in Turgot's government. 'You are fortunate,' says hapless Louis gloomily, 'to be able to resign. I wish I could.' The storm was coming up fast. But the first man on whom it was to fall remained calm and staunch.
On April 30, 1776, Turgot wrote to his King a note begging him not to appoint Amelot as Malesherbes' successor, and containing these ominous words: 'Do not forget, Sire, that it was weakness that brought the head of Charles the First to the block.' Louis made no answer. Finally, the match was put to the tinder of the Queen's wrath by Turgot's dismissal from office of her worthless protégé, de Guines; and the Minister, it was whispered, had also declined to pay a debt she had incurred for jewellery, as against the new rules he had himself made. Rules for a Queen! This must certainly be the end of Queens or of Ministers! In this case, it was the end of both; only Turgot's fall came first.
As he was sitting writing, on May 12, 1776, Bertin arrived to announce to him that he was no longer Controller-General. He had been drawing up an edict; laying down his pen he observed quietly, 'My successor will finish it.' His successor, it has been well said, was the National Assembly.
Two days later, Marie Antoinette wrote exultantly to her mother of his dismissal. What did she care for the just reproaches of the King and of the whole nation, which that old killjoy, Mercy Argenteau, declared that this deed would bring on her head? She would have liked her enemy turned out of office and sent to the Bastille the very day that de Guines was made a Duke. Poor Queen! Her little triumph was so short, and her bitter punishment so long!
On May 18, Turgot took farewell of his master in language nobly dignified and touching. 'My one desire,' he said, 'is that

VIII: TURGOT: THE STATESMAN

you may find I have judged wrongly, that I have warned you of imaginary dangers.'

Clugny was appointed Controller-General; *corvée* and *jurandes* were re-established; the edict establishing free trade in grain was revoked. The Court rejoiced aloud; the Paris Parliament was delighted. Old Voltaire at Ferney, indeed, wept and said that this was death before death, that a thunderbolt had fallen on his head and his heart; and the wise knew that nothing could save France now.

Turgot retired quietly into private life. That he was disappointed, not for himself, but for his country, is very true. True, too, he was angered at the backstairs policy which had dismissed him. But far beyond this, there was so much he could have done, which now he could never do! Faithful to his life-long principle of gathering up the fragments that remain, he read and studied much, corresponded with Hume and Adam Smith, often met and talked with Franklin, went to see Voltaire when he came to Paris in 1778, made experiments in chemistry and physics, and was active in private benevolence. Was the brief evening of his life solitary? The one human affection which, in its perfection, makes loneliness impossible, was not his; or at best was his only as a dream or a memory. But in the great family of earth's toiling children he must have known there were many to love and bless him, many he had saved from wrong or from sorrow, some whom he had made from beasts into men. Another blessing was his—he did not long survive his active labours. He died March 21, 1781, aged fifty-four.

A failure, this life? It may be so; but a failure beside which many a success is paltry.

Turgot could not save France from her Revolution, but he gave her, and all countries, practical, working theories on government, on the liberty of the press, on the best means of helping the poor, on the use of riches, on civil, political, and religious liberty, which are still invaluable.

He has been justly said to have founded modern political economy; to have bequeathed to future generations 'the idea of the freedom of industry;' and to have made ready the way for the reforms which are the glory of our own day.

Among Voltaire's fellow-workers there are far more dazzling personalities. But from their fiery words, exalted visions, and too glorious hopes one turns with a certain sense of relief to this quiet, strong, practical man, and understands why the people, whose instinct in judging the character of their rulers seldom betrays them in the long run, specially acclaimed Turgot as a friend.

IX: BEAUMARCHAIS: THE PLAYWRIGHT

Some men do great things incidentally and unintentionally. Pierre Augustin Caron de Beaumarchais bothered his clever head scarcely at all with schemes for the well-being of his country—was little concerned with humanity and very much with one man—himself. Yet by a special irony of destiny the author of 'The Marriage of Figaro' played one of the chief parts in the prelude to the drama of the Revolution.

Born in Paris on January 24, 1732, the son of a watchmaker with a large family, Pierre Augustin Caron early learnt his father's trade, picked up a little Latin at a technical school at Alfort and the rest of his education from experience and from the world.

A lively, impudent, good-looking boy, young Caron was from the first clever with that smart cleverness which is as distinct from genius or from wisdom, as kindness is distinct from sympathy. He was as sharp over his watchmaking as over everything he undertook in life. He had his first lawsuit—the first of so many!—over a discovery he made in his trade, and won it. But he was young, gay, musical, and Parisian. His trade was only a part of his life. There were debts and escapades. Then the watches took to disappearing mysteriously out of old Caron's shop; and finally old Caron turned his scapegrace out of doors, till the mother pleaded, not in vain, for the prodigal's return.

Then the prodigal made the loveliest and smallest of watches for Madame de Pompadour's ring. The King was pleased to desire one also, and the King's daughters, Mesdames, followed their father's example; while the courtiers could not, of course, be out of the fashion. Pierre Caron, tall, handsome, audacious, was presented at Versailles, and made watchmaker to his Majesty. In 1755, another piece of luck befell him. (This Caron was one of the luckiest of human beings all through his life.)

A pretty young married woman, who had noticed him admiringly at Versailles, came to his shop to have her watch mended. Caron took it back to her house in person. A few months later the charming person's elderly husband sold to Caron his post at Court, and on November 9, 1755, a patent was accorded to the watchmaker's son declaring him 'one of the Clerk Controllers of the Pantry of our Household.' An agreeable little post, this of Pharaoh's butler. Nothing to do, only be sure you do it handsomely! Caron, looking exceedingly effective and magnificent, preceded the King's roast with a sword clanking at his side. At the end of a few months his predecessor in this arduous occupation died, and young Caron married the charming widow, Madame Francquet, who was certainly older than himself, but not the less agreeable to a very young man for that.

His marriage could not, at least, have been one of interest; or he was so far disinterested that he neglected to complete the marriage settlements, and when Madame Caron died, in ten months' time, Caron found himself penniless. She had, it is said, a very small property, but it was apparently so small as to be invisible, for no one has ever discovered its whereabouts. But it is memorable as having suggested to Caron the name by which he now called himself, and has been ever since known —Beaumarchais.

In a very short time the young widower (he was only twenty-five) reappeared at Versailles, not as a watchmaker or butler, but as a musician.

All the social talents had Caron—tact, impudence, a witty tongue, a delightful voice, added to a real talent for the harp, which was the fashionable instrument of the moment. Mesdames killed a great deal of the too ample royal leisure with music; Madame Adelaide played every instrument down to the horn and the comb. This delightful young *parvenu* is the very man to teach us the harp! He not only did that, but he organised concerts, of which he was himself the bright, particular star.

On one occasion the King was so impatient for him to begin to play, that he pushed towards him his own armchair; while on another, Mesdames declined the present of a fan on which the painter had portrayed their concerts—without the figure of Beaumarchais. Of course the courtiers were jealous. The beautiful insolence of his manners, the perfectly good-natured conceit (surely one of the most exasperating of the minor vices) naturally made him enemies. One scornful young noble handed this new favourite, this royal instructor, his watch to look at.

'Sir,' says Beaumarchais, 'since I have given up my trade I have become very awkward in such matters.'

'Do not refuse me, I beg.'

Beaumarchais takes the watch, pretends to examine it, and

IX: BEAUMARCHAIS: THE PLAYWRIGHT

drops it. 'Sir,' says he, with a bow to the owner, 'I warned you of my clumsiness,' and, turning on his heel, leaves the watch in fragments on the floor.

The new courtier was at least a match for the old ones. 'I was born to be a courtier,' says Figaro. 'To accept, to take, and to ask; there is the secret in three words.' Figaro's father had the secret already. Soon he made friends with Paris-Duverney, financier and Court banker, 'asked' of him the art of making money, and 'received' so much of it that in 1761 he could buy himself a brevet of nobility. He would have bought also the post of Master of Woods and Forests, but that the other Masters objected so lustily to receiving such a *bourgeois* into their order, that even the patronage of Mesdames, and his own wit displayed in an amusing pamphlet, could not gain the bourgeois his point. So he bought the post of Lieutenant-General of the King's Preserves instead, and in that capacity sat solemnly in a long robe once a week in judgment on the poachers of the neighbourhood of Paris.

In 1764, he made a journey into Spain, where one of his sisters, who had married a Spaniard, was living, and another had just been jilted with a peculiar insolence and brutality by a man called Clavijo. Beaumarchais brought Clavijo to book; the day of the wedding was fixed, when the shifty suitor absconded a second time. Beaumarchais made the episode famous in his account of the affair, which appeared in his Fourth Memoir against Goezman in February 1774, and which naturally does not tend to the discredit of M. Pierre Augustin Caron.

Besides protecting his sister and exposing her betrayer, this energetic person was carrying out a secret mission from Duverney and recovering bad debts of old Caron's. Then, too, he was enormously enjoying Spanish society, and writing love-letters to a pretty Creole, Pauline, whom he had left in Paris and whom he may magnificently condescend to marry if her estates in St. Domingo really turn out to be worth consideration. He was further corresponding with Voltaire, and, richest and most fruitful of all his Spanish transactions, studying the Spanish stage.

He came home in 1765. After his return, he appeared, in 1767, as a playwright, making his debut in one of those heavy and tearful dramas in the unfortunate style of Diderot's 'Natural Son.' No one reads or acts 'Eugenie' now; but when the adaptable Caron had shortened and altered it, it mildly pleased the playgoing Parisians for a few evenings.

In 1768, Beaumarchais married another widow, Madame

Lévêque, having abandoned Pauline, or having been abandoned by her on the score of his mercenariness. Madame Lévêque was rich and young, and when she suddenly died three years later there were not wanting envious enemies to accuse this aspiring Caron of having poisoned both his wives. The fact that their deaths left him the poorer might have exonerated him, if his own character did not; but, as Voltaire said—Voltaire, who was watching his rise in the world with a keen interest, and who rarely made a mistake in judging human nature—'A quick, impetuous, passionate man like Beaumarchais gives a wife a blow, or even two wives two blows, but he does not poison them.'
It may be noted, moreover, that all the women who touched his life adored this Caron. He was so handsome and good-natured and successful! A little selfish certainly; but some women seem to love that quality in a man—it gives them so great a scope for denying themselves. And then he was always so brave and gay!
His success now deserted him for a little while. He offended the King by suggesting a *mot* with a meaning—Figaro, it seems, was getting apt in them already—which a duke gave forth at one of the little suppers of Madame Dubarry and which displeased his Majesty, who, to be sure, had reason to dread hidden meanings.
Then came the affair Goezman.
In 1770 Duverney died, and Beaumarchais immediately quarrelled with his heir, the Comte de la Blache, and plunged into a lawsuit over a sum of fifteen thousand francs. Beaumarchais won the first move in the game. But unluckily he had more than one iron in the fire just then. He fell out fiercely with the Duc de Chaulnes over a Mademoiselle Mesnard, with the result that the Duke was clapped into a fortress, and Beaumarchais into the prison of For-l'Évêque. La Blache seized his opportunity, brought his lawsuit before the Parliament of Paris, represented dumb and imprisoned Beaumarchais as the greatest scoundrel unhanged, won his cause, seized Beaumarchais' furniture, and entirely ruined him.
Beaumarchais seldom lost his coolness and courage, and he did not lose them now. While in Por-l'Évêque he had been let out on leave three or four times. He had taken these chances to try to win over to his side Goezman, who was Judge-Reporter in the lawsuit with la Blache, and a most unfavourable judge to Beaumarchais. By the simple and time-honoured expedient

of handsome bribes to the wife, Beaumarchais attempted to gain the husband's good will. Madame Goezman perfectly understands that, should Beaumarchais lose his cause, she is to return his gifts of a watch, set in diamonds, and of money. The cause is lost. She returns the watch and money, save only a certain fifteen louis, to which, for some absurd *raisonnement de femme*, she considers herself entitled, and with which she will by no means part. Then Councillor Goezman comes forward and accuses M. de Beaumarchais of seeking to corrupt his integrity.

This ridiculous situation Beaumarchais seized as a golden opportunity to restore his credit before the world, to dazzle it with his wit, to entice it with his audacity, and to make it own him the man of matchless cleverness he was. He appealed to public opinion, nominally to judge between himself and Goezman, in reality to judge between him, Goezman, la Blache, the Paris Parliament, and all his enemies and rivals whomsoever, in four famous Memoirs, which, divided Paris into two hostile camps and fixed on him the delighted attention of Europe.

Except by name, and for a brilliant quotation here and there, few people know the Goezman Memoirs now. But in fire, wit, and irony, they are little, if at all, inferior to the comedies by which Beaumarchais lives. In both are the same gay surprises of situation, banter and mockery, parry and thrust—every page as light and elusive as thistledown borne on a summer breeze. Their cleverness gained him the admiration not only of a senile King, but of Voltaire as well. Old Ferney declared he had never been so much amused in his life. 'What a man!' he wrote to d'Alembert. 'He has all the qualities;' and again, 'Don't tell *me* he has poisoned his wife, he is much too lively and amusing for that.'

Madame Dubarry had charades acted in her apartment, in which an interview between Beaumarchais and Madame Goezman was represented on the stage. The Memoirs were read aloud in the cafés. Of the Fourth, six thousand copies were sold in a single day. Horace Walpole delighted in them. Madame du Deffand gossiped of them. Bernardin de Saint-Pierre prophesied for Beaumarchais the reputation of Molière. What did it avail then, on February 26, 1774, when the case had lasted some three years, to give judgment against him, sentence him to civic degradation, prohibit him from the occupation of any public function, and condemn the Memoirs to be burnt as scandalous, libellous, defamatory? He was the victor not the less. 'Le monde a beau parler, il faut obéir,' says Voltaire. The day after the sentence had been pronounced, the Prince de Conti and the Duc de Chartres fêted the criminal, and a delightful woman fell in love with him. Marie Antoinette named her latest coiffure after a joke in the Memoirs. He was so wildly applauded when he appeared in public that Sartine, the Lieutenant of Police, advised him to appear no more. 'It is not enough to be condemned,' says Sartine, 'one should be a little modest still.' The Maupeou Parliament in attempting to destroy this wit had ruined itself. Its ban was worse than useless. Beaumarchais was the fashion. The King, to be sure, had to enjoin silence on this 'terrible advocate,' but he promised him a revision of his suit; and then employed him, in March, 1774, as his secret agent in England to run to earth a person who had threatened to publish a scandalous pamphlet on Madame Dubarry. Beaumarchais succeeded in his mission. He always succeeded. But when he returned to France, Louis the Fifteenth was dying, so for all his pains his reward was, as he said, 'swollen legs and an empty purse.'

Soon, however, news came of a libel against Marie Antoinette which was being prepared in London. Off starts Beaumarchais again, pursues the libeller (a shifty Jew) to Nüremberg, goes on to Vienna to procure from Maria Theresa an extradition treaty against him, is himself thrown into prison for a month, and then liberated with profusest apologies and the offer of a thousand ducats. All his adventures were delightfully romantic and picturesque; and with his eye for scenic effect, he took care they should lose nothing in the telling.

A year later, in 1775, he came to England on another and far more important secret mission connected with the rebellion of the American colonies. It was the one enterprise of his life, it is said, into which he put more heart than head. He attended parliamentary debates, and was constantly at the house of Wilkes. 'All sensible people in England,' he wrote to Louis the Sixteenth in September 1775, 'are convinced that the English colonies are lost.' He advised that, while France should not openly embroil herself with England, she should send secret aid to the insurgents. For this purpose, financed by his country, he equipped for war three ships—his 'navy' he called it—and when he returned to Paris he traded in the American interest under the name of Roderigue, Hortalez & Co. England was naturally angry when she found out how she had been tricked, and America, so far as money

IX: BEAUMARCHAIS: THE PLAYWRIGHT

acknowledgments were concerned, was not a little ungrateful. But the clever instrument, Beaumarchais, came out of the affair with his usual flourish and distinction, and would have deserved a paragraph in history, even had he not earned a page in literature.

On February 23, 1775, there was produced at the old Comédie Française in the Rue des Fossés, Saint-Germain des Prés, opposite the famous Café Procope, a play called 'The Barber of Seville.'

Accepted by the Comédie Frangaise in 1772, its first performance, fixed for Shrove Tuesday 1773, had been stopped by the authorities because just at that moment its author was unluckily serving a term of imprisonment for fighting the Duc de Chaulnes. Before the next date fixed for its debut, he had been condemned by the Maupeou Parliament for the affair with la Blache. The third attempt was no luckier. The irrepressible creature had just published the Fourth Goezman Memoir!

And now, when the performance really did come off, it was a failure. La Harpe declared that its inordinate length bored people, its bad jokes irritated them, and its false morality shocked them. The *parterre* was loudly and vulgarly disgusted, and the boxes yawned behind their fans. By Beaumarchais? He was but mediocre before, we remember, in 'Eugenie.' Watchmaker, courtier, advocate, secret agent, this—but clearly no playwright!

In twenty-four hours Caron had laid violent hands on his 'Barber,' shortened him, enlivened him, cut out his distasteful jokes and his dubious moralities, and 'under the pressure of a discontented and disappointed public' turned him into a masterpiece. At its second performance the play was applauded to the skies. It ran through the whole winter season. It delighted its author to print it with its title-page running: 'The Barber of Seville, Comedy in Four Acts, represented and failed at the Comédie Française.' It drew on him one of his dear lawsuits, and enabled him to place the rights of dramatists over their works on a new and firm basis, and to found the first Society of Dramatic Authors. Far above all, it led the way to 'Figaro.'

The subject of 'The Barber of Seville' is the time-honoured one of the amorous old guardian who falls in love with his ward; only Beaumarchais' guardian is a wit, not a fool. It is the defect, indeed, of both his great plays that all the characters are wits. He fell into Sheridan's fault, and made his *personæ*

the mouthpieces of his own cleverness. He wholly lacked the far higher and finer genius, the exquisite fidelity to life and character, which made Shakespeare give to each of his creatures the special kind of cleverness, and no other, proper to its nature.
Not the less, Beaumarchais writes with a lightness and effervescence which are without counterpart in dramatic literature. 'The Barber of Seville' was taken, it is said, from an opera of Sedaine's, and was itself originally designed to be a comic opera. Nothing but a quarrel with the composer of the score prevented it from first appearing in that form in which it is to-day most familiar to the world.
Yet it hardly needs an accompaniment of lively music. The airs and the singing are there already—in the gay *bizarrerie* of situation, the laughing swing of repartee, and the brilliant recitative of the longer speeches. The characters, called by Spanish names and dressed in Spanish clothes, are thoroughly and essentially French. Its exquisite delicacy of touch and its rippling mocking gaiety declare it, in fact, not only the work of a Frenchman, but one of the most Gallic pieces that have ever held the stage. It inaugurated a new order of comedy, and introduced into it a new character: the Barber, who was also wit, hero, and moralist—the character of Figaro.
Beaumarchais was not at all the man to sit down and tranquilly enjoy his first dramatic triumph. He must not only follow it up by writing another, but he must with enormous difficulty, at the risk of much money, and three years' hard work, become the editor of the first complete edition of Voltaire's works ever given to the public.
Then, too, he must prepare the reorganisation of the *ferme générale* with the Minister, Vergennes. Actresses consulted him when they were out of an engagement, and dramatic authors when their liberties were endangered. The author of the Goezman Memoirs can surely help a poor simpleton engulfed in a lawsuit, and the friend of Duverney, the rich man who began the world in a tradesman's shop, may well assist a ruined speculator! Inventors, impatient to air their discoveries, carried them to him who had brought his first legal action over a discovery of his own. Girls deceived by their lovers begged the assistance of the man who had held up Clavijo to infamy.
One of the most fortunate characteristics Beaumarchais possessed was his power of suddenly changing his occupation, and one of his most extraordinary characteristics

was his love of doing so. 'Shutting the drawer of an affair,' he himself called this faculty. He shut the drawer with a bang, and perfectly good-natured, self-conceited, and successful, turned from a secret agency in London to interfere with the marriage of the Prince of Nassau, and from the marriage to assist the Lieutenant of the Police in censuring the works of his brother-playwrights, and from that censorship to put into the mouth of Figaro such sentiments as, 'Printed follies are without importance except in those places where their circulation is forbidden … without the liberty to blame no praise can be flattering.'
By 1778, 'The Marriage of Figaro' was finished; and in 1781 it was received by the Comédie Française. But it contained that which no censor—not even dull Louis—could pass. In 1782, he read it, and flung it from him. 'This is detestable, this shall never be played!'
But that prohibition was not enough for Beaumarchais. Forbidden fruit is ever the most tantalising and delicious. Daintily tied with pink ribbons he sent a copy of the play to this salon; and another to that. He announced a reading of it— and, coquettishly and without offering any reason, abandoned the reading at the last moment. In a little while he had raised all Paris on the tip-toe of excitement. Not to have scanned at least a scene or two of 'The Marriage of Figaro' was to confess oneself out of the fashion. Then the author read the whole of it to the Grand Duke of Russia, and recited selections of it to the Comtesse de Lamballe and to Marshal Richelieu, 'before bishops and archbishops.'
After all, Louis was very weak, and public opinion very strong. The First Gentleman of the Chamber permitted the thing to be rehearsed, more or less publicly, in the theatre of the Hôtel des Menus Plaisirs. All the world and his wife crowded thitlhr. The Comte d'Artois was actually on his way when, with an awakening of his feeble obstinacy, the King sent a mandate forbidding the performance. Even Madame de Campan, kindly old sycophant of the Court, confessed that there were angry whispers of 'tyranny' and 'oppression,' and murmurs of 'an attack on liberty.' Beaumarchais, stung to the quick, swore that it should be played, ay, even if it was in the choir of Notre-Dame! The pressure on Louis was great; the Court was in want of a new sensation, and to be made to laugh at its own follies was a very new one indeed.
In three months, the Comte de Vaudreuil, the leader of Marie Antoinette's *société intime* of the Little Trianon, obtained the

royal permission to have it acted in his house at Gennevilliers, by the company from the Comédie, before the Comte d'Artois and the Queen's bosom friend, the Duchesse de Polignac. The Queen herself intended to have been present, but was prevented by an indisposition. When the permission was accorded, Beaumarchais was in England. He hurried home, saw to the performance himself, and made his own conditions.

On September 26, 1783, three hundred persons, the very flower of Court society, crowded into Vaudreuil's theatre, and would have died of suffocation if the resourceful Beaumarchais had not broken the panes of the windows with his cane. It was said he had made a hit in two senses. The aristocratic audience received his play with rapturous applause. He adroitly followed up his success by presenting his piece to a tribunal of censors who, for some unknown reason, 'felt sure it would be a failure,' and expressed themselves satisfied with it after they had made a few insignificant omissions. Finally, a reluctant permission was wrung from the King, and on April 27, 1784, seven months after the performance at Gennevilliers, 'The Marriage of Figaro' was first publicly performed at the new Comédie Française, built on the site of the Hôtel de Condé, and now known as the Odéon.

The play was to begin at half-past five in the afternoon, but from early in the morning the doors were besieged by crowds, in which *cordons bleus* elbowed Savoyards, and the classes and the masses began their long struggle. In the press three persons were suffocated—'one more than for Scudéry,' said caustic La Harpe. Great ladies sat all day in the dressing rooms of the actresses to be sure of securing seats, and duchesses were delighted to obtain a footstool in the gallery, a part of the house to which, as a rule, ladies never went. The theatre was lit by a new method. The famous Dazincourt played Figaro; and Molé, Almaviva. The author himself was in a private box between two abbés who had promised to administer 'very spiritual succour' in case of death. Then the curtain rose.

'The "Marriage of Figaro,"' said Napoleon, 'was the Revolution already in action.'

As in the 'Barber of Seville,' the atmosphere and the clothes are Spanish, the spirit and essence wholly French. The story of Figaro, the servant who outwits his lord and wins Suzanne, whom his master has tried to steal from him, forms a plot simple enough. Count Almaviva, the master, is certainly one of the best representations of the great noble of the old regime ever put on the stage. Continually worsted in argument by his valet, and perpetually in the most ridiculous situations, he never loses the dignity of good breeding—as Beaumarchais himself puts it, 'the corruption of his heart takes nothing from the *bon ton* of his manners.' Figaro is, of course, democracy with its wits awake at last, and stung to courage and action by centuries of wrongs. The Countess (the Rosina of the 'Barber') and Suzanne are the most charming and seductive reproductions of the eighteenth-century woman—'spirituelles et rieuses,' coquettish, graceful and gay. The chief fault of the play is the episode of Marceline, in which the playgoer wearily recognises two, too familiar friends—the long-lost mother and the mislaid baby with the usual convenient birth-mark on the right arm.

The morals of the piece are throughout the morals of the time—indelicacy, delicately expressed. Figaro hardly ever says anything *inconvenant*, but intrigue is in the very air he breathes. 'The ripening fruit,' writes Saint-Amand, 'hanging on the tree, never falls but seems always on the point of falling.' Virtue, of a kind, does triumph in the long run, but Beaumarchais knew his audience so well that up to the last moment he kept them fearing, or hoping, that it would not. If its unpleasant situations, and the character of the precocious page Cherubino (a particularly distasteful one to English ideas), gave spice to the wit in its own day, the modern reader can enjoy the sparkling and rippling stream of mocking gaiety without stirring up the mud it hides. One situation leads to another with the most complete naturalness, and yet that other is always perfectly unexpected. Moralisings and soliloquies, which spell ruin in other plays, are in this one rich in brilliancy and aptness. Those who as yet know 'The Marriage of Figaro' only by name, can purchase for a few pence one of the most exhilarating draughts of intellectual champagne ever given to the world.

But it is not only as literature that the play lives. It *was* the Revolution already in action. There are hardly six consecutive lines which do not contain some indictment against the old order; there is not an aphorism which does not push, with a laugh, some abuse down the abyss. 'There is one thing more amazing than my play,' said Beaumarchais, 'and that is its success.' He was right. One can but marvel still that the old order, so clearly hearing its sentence of death, took that

sentence only as a stupendous joke, 'laughed its last laugh' over 'Figaro,' and applauded the warrant for its own execution till its hands tingled again.
The fine ladies heard their vapours defined as 'the malady that prevails only in boudoirs;' and my lord, surrounded by sycophants, saw himself for a mocking second as other men see him, when Figaro says to Bazile: 'Are you a Prince to be flattered? Hear the truth, wretch, since you have not the money to pay a liar.'
With what a roar of laughter that tribunal of censors who had licensed the play heard the words: 'Provided I do not mention in my writings, authority, religion, politics, morality, officials … or anyone who has a claim to anything, I can print everything freely under the inspection of two or three censors;' and with what amused self-complacency it listened to the axiom: 'Only little minds fear little writings.'
The hereditary noble listened to this: 'Nobility, money, rank, place, all that makes people so proud! What have you done for so much good fortune? You have given yourself the trouble to be born;' and the *bourgeois* at his side, to whom merit had opened no path to glory, heard with a strange thrill Figaro continue, 'While for me, lost in a crowd of nobodies, I have had need of more knowledge and calculation simply to exist, than has been employed to govern all the Spains for a hundred years.'
Did the Minister who had filled the snug posts in the Government with his own relations and friends see nothing but a joke in: 'They thought of me for a situation, but unluckily I was fit for it; they wanted an accountant; a dancer obtained the place'? 'Intelligence a help to advancement? Your lordship is laughing at mine. Be commonplace and cringing, and you can get anywhere.' 'To succeed in life, *le savoir-faire vaut mieux que le savoir.*'
The ubiquitous Englishman of the audience heard Figaro announce 'Goddam' to be 'the basis of the English language.' The political world listened to a scathing definition of diplomacy: 'To pretend to be ignorant of what everyone else knows, and to know what everyone else does not know … to seem deep when one is only empty and hollow … to set spies and pension traitors … to break seals and intercept letters … there's diplomacy, or I'm a dead man.'
The audience trooped out into the night—the performance lasted from half-past five till ten—with enthusiastic admiration on its lips and still ringing in its ears the seventh

couplet of the vaudeville:
>Par le sort de la naissance,
>L'un est roi, l'autre est berger;
>Le hasard fit leur distance;
>L'esprit seul peut tout changer.

The writer, certainly, had as little idea as his audience that his was to be the wit to change everything. From first to last, Beaumarchais was the man we have always with us, who means to advance in the world and let that world take care of itself; whose argument is that posterity having done nothing for him, he need do nothing for posterity; the true time-server, just audacious enough to say what less courageous people only dare to think, and earning thereby their gratitude and applause. Caron had reaped place and fortune from the old order, and was not at all minded to overthrow it. Tyranny for tyranny, he preferred the despotism of the King to the despotism of the mob. If he revenged himself in his play for the slights and humiliations from which even his cleverness had not been able to save him—that was absolutely all. Overturn Throne and Church! Such a *bouleversement* would very likely overturn Caron de Beaumarchais too, and was not to be thought of.

Yet it was this man who gave light popular expression to the principles to which Voltaire and his friends devoted their lives, their ardour, and their genius. It was surely a cruelty of fate that the Master could not live to see 'Figaro.' Its author might miss its significance, but Voltaire—never.

Beaumarchais, indeed, had merely caught the accent of his age, as a child catches the accent of its nurse, and 'wrote revolutionary literature, as M. Jourdain spoke prose, without knowing it.' In 'The Marriage of Figaro' he said what all men were feeling, but not what he felt. He wished to be a successful playwright, and he was one; but he did not mean to be one of the greatest and most influential of Revolutionists—and he was that too.

He followed up the success of 'The Marriage of Figaro' by generously founding a fashionable charity, to be known later as the Benevolent Maternal Institution, and the King followed up the success he had always disliked by punishing an imprudent letter Caron had written in a newspaper, and which had offended Monsieur, by writing on a playing card, as he sat at his game, an order for Beaumarchais' imprisonment.

By one of those charming little surprises for which the old *régime* was so celebrated, Beaumarchais, of fifty-three, found himself locked up in St. Lazare, then a house of correction for juvenile offenders. At first Paris went into roars of laughter, and then she became very angry indeed. In a few days she obtained the release of her playwright; and Louis, with the inconceivable inconsistency that distinguished his career, not only gave him enormous monetary compensation, but permitted as a further reparation, 'The Barber of Seville' to be played at the Little Trianon.

That representation marked the crowning point of Beaumarchais' success. Dazincourt trained the company of royal and noble amateurs. Marie Antoinette was rehearsing the part of Rosina with Madame de Campan when she first heard of the opening of a grimmer drama, the scandal of the Diamond Necklace. On August 15, 1785, Cardinal de Rohan was arrested. On the 19th, 'The Barber of Seville' was played in the theatre of the Little Trianon, with lucky Beaumarchais in the audience, the Queen as Rosina, the Comte de Vaudreuil as Almaviva, the Duc de Guiche as Bartholo, and the Comte d'Artois as Figaro.

The Queen was infinitely vivacious in her part. Did Bazile's terrible definition of Calumny disconcert her?

'At first a mere breath, skimming the ground like a swallow, but sowing poison as it flies ... it takes root, creeps up, makes its way, goes ... from mouth to mouth: then, all of a sudden, one knows not how, Calumny is standing upright, rearing its head, hissing, swelling, growing visibly. It spreads its wings, takes flight, eddies round ... bursts, thunders, crashes, and becomes, thanks to heaven, a general outcry, a public crescendo, a universal chorus of hatred and proscription. What devil could resist it?'

If Queen or audience found in the words too awful an application and prophecy, history does not relate.

How strange, with the knowledge of after events, sound in the mouth of d'Artois the words: 'I am happy to be forgotten, being sure that a great man does enough good when he does no harm. As to the virtues one requires in a servant, does your Excellency know many masters who are worthy of being valets?' and, most strange of all, 'I hasten to laugh at everything, lest I should have to weep at everything.'

The performance of the 'Barber' at Trianon was the last flicker of the dying fire of royal pleasure. Beaumarchais' own light began to fail. He was shortly involved in a famous dispute

with Mirabeau about the Paris Water Company, in which that great genius brought out his mighty guns of irony and invective and in one fierce blast blew, as it were, Beaumarchais' nimble-witted head from his shoulders. 'Figaro' has dubbed my diatribes 'Mirabelles,' has he? Well, he shall pun at my expense no more. All Paris stood watching. Dazzling, burning, and terrible, Mirabeau's sun was rising above the horizon, and Beaumarchais' star was fading in the stormy sky. Then he had another lawsuit, in which he entered the lists as the champion of wronged beauty. His opponent was Bergasse, the young lawyer, who 'had his reputation to make' at some one's expense, and made it at Beaumarchais'.
In 1786, Caron married Mademoiselle Willermaula, who had long been his mistress, and by whom he had a daughter, Eugénie. For them, he built a splendid house looking on to the Bastille, near the Porte Saint-Antoine, which became one of the sights of Paris.
In 1787, he produced a very feeble opera, 'Tarare,' which had a small temporary success.
On July 14, 1789, the Bastille fell. Not only the fine house was in danger, but its fine owner as well. He had written 'Figaro'? Yes. But he had been the courtier and the secret agent of kings. His pluck and energy did not in the least desert him. In the midst of the uproar he was writing a new play, 'The Guilty Mother.'
La Harpe (no wonder his friends called him La Harpie) declared it was 'downright silly;' and perhaps this thorough-going verdict is but little too severe. 'The Guilty Mother' forms a sort of third volume to the 'Barber' and 'Figaro,' and falls as flat as most sequels. The same characters appear, grown old. The Guilty Mother is the Rosina of the 'Barber' and the Countess Almaviva of 'Figaro;' while Cherubino has grown up into the very objectionable young man such a boy *would* grow into. Beaumarchais had built a theatre—the Théâtre du Marais—near his house, in which he proposed his new piece should appear.
On June 6, 1792, the day before it was to be produced, its author was denounced before the National Assembly by Chabot. He had indeed, with a view to making at once a *coup* for his country and for himself, and though he was now sixty years old and getting deaf, undertaken to bring into France sixty thousand guns—'to massacre patriots,' shouted unreasonable patriotism. On August 10 his house was searched; on August 23 he was taken to the Abbaye prison,

and on August 30 he was freed by Manuel (his brother *littérateur*, as well as Procurator of the Commune), just two days before the September massacres. After all, his star had not yet declined.

After hiding in barns and roaming 'over harrowed fields, panting for his life,' he escaped to England, where very luckily for himself a London merchant, to whom he was in debt, prevented his returning to Paris and the guillotine by shutting him up in the King's Bench Prison. In March, 1793, he did return, 'to offer my head to the sword of justice, if I cannot prove I am a good citizen,' That he did not thus pay for his imprudence proves that there was as much in that head as had ever come out of it.

Three months later, Beaumarchais was sent as the emissary of the Revolutionary Government to fetch those sixty thousand guns which had been left in Holland. He had many highly dramatic escapes and adventures; and, being wholly modern in his belief in self-advertisement, he once more made the most of them. In his absence the Government which had sent him, by one of those little mistakes which make its history so vivacious, declared him an *émigré!*

During the Terror he was at Hamburg, in direst poverty and in mortal anxiety as to the fate of his wife, his daughter, and his sister Julie. They escaped with their lives; but when Beaumarchais was at last taken off the list of *émigrés* and returned to Paris in 1796, he found house and fortune alike in ruins, his door besieged by creditors, and his famous garden a wilderness.

He was sixty-four years old and had already done more in his life than a hundred ordinary men compress into a hundred ordinary careers. And now he must start afresh!

He saw his daughter married; revived his old social tastes, produced 'The Guilty Mother,' and took the keenest interest, both in prose and verse, in that young Lieutenant of Artillery, Napoleon Bonaparte. He also published two very anti-Christian letters in praise of Voltaire. The watchmaker's son, who had charmed Mesdames at Versailles, was to the end witty, gay, bold, and practical.

On the morning of May 18, 1799, his friends found him dead of apoplexy. To die in his bed at last was surely not the least of his clevernesses.

Caron de Beaumarchais was not a very unusual type of character or even of intellect; but in the use he made of his brains, of his qualities and of his circumstances, he was a man

IX: BEAUMARCHAIS: THE PLAYWRIGHT

in a million. His marvellous enterprise and industry enabled him to build more than one successful career on very ordinary foundations. His luck, that astonishing luck which followed him from the cradle to the grave, seems to have prevented such dangerous qualities as his conceit, his pugnaciousness, and his love of intrigue and speculation, from bringing their usual fatal results. Such gifts as a handsome face, a fine figure, a 'parvenu grandeur of manner' and real kindness and generosity, he used to their utmost advantage. For himself and his contemporaries he was a brilliantly successful individuality.

For posterity, he is the man who, with a single thrust, pushed open that door, which by long labour and bitter sacrifice Voltaire and the Encyclopædists had unbarred, upon the great Revolution and the Day.

X: CONDORCET: THE ARISTOCRAT

Voltaire was the son of a lawyer, and Diderot the son of a cutler; d'Alembert was a no-man's child educated in a tradesman's family; Grimm and Galiani were foreigners in the country to which they gave their talents. Of all Voltaire's fellowship only Vauvenargues and Condorcet came from the order their work was pledged not to benefit but to destroy. Condorcet alone lived to experience the extreme consequences of his principles, and paid for them by imprisonment and death. The Aristocrat who lost his life through the People to whom he had devoted it—this was Jean Antoine Nicolas de Caritat, Marquis de Condorcet.

Born in 1743, at Ribemont, a town in Picardy, Condorcet belonged to a noble family highly connected both with the Church and the Army.

His father was a captain of cavalry and designed his son for the same aristocratic post. But he died when the child was four; and a devout mother vowed him to the Virgin and *au blanc*, dressed him in white frocks like a little girl, so that the luckless Caritat could neither run nor jump as nature bade him, and owed to his mother's piety a weakness in his limbs from which he never recovered.

His first schoolmasters were the Jesuits. What is one to make of the fact that they had as virgin soil the intellects of at least four of their mightiest and fiercest opponents—Voltaire, Diderot, Turgot, and Condorcet?

At eleven, Caritat was under their supervision, with his home influence pressing him to their way of thought, with an uncle a bishop, and Cardinal de Bernis a relative. At thirteen, he was sent to Rheims, to be more completely under their control. At fifteen, he came up to Paris, and began at the College of Navarre to study mathematics and to think for himself; and when once a mind has begun to do that, nothing can stop it. His treatment of a particularly difficult theme brought him the acquaintance of d'Alembert, who first saw in the boy, who was to be to him as a son, a kindred genius, a future colleague at the Academy. Caritat was only seventeen when he introduced himself to his other great friend, Turgot, writing him a 'Letter on Justice and Virtue' which already proclaimed this college student a thinker of a high order. An 'Essay on the

X: CONDORCET: THE ARISTOCRAT

Integral Calculus,' which he presented at the Academy of Sciences when he was twenty-two, attracted to him the flattering notice of the famous mathematician, Lagrange. There was in it not only the ardour of youth and a buoyant fecundity of idea, but a profundity of learning not at all youthful.

Caritat was now no longer a student, but still lodging in Paris. In 1769, when he was twenty-six, he entered the Academy of Sciences in opposition to the wishes of all his relatives, who never pardoned him, he said, for not becoming a captain of cavalry.

The man who ought, by the solemn unwritten laws of the family compact, to have been a heavy dragoon, was soon acknowledged as one of the finest original thinkers of his age, the friend of d'Alembert and of Voltaire, and something yet greater than a thinker—greater than any great man's friend—a practical reformer and a generous lover of human-kind.

The character of Condorcet—he who with Turgot has been said to have been 'the highest intellectual and moral personality of his century'—has in it much not only infinitely good, but also infinitely attractive. Perfectly simple and modest, somewhat shy in the social world which he himself defined as 'dissipation without pleasure, vanity without motive, and idleness without rest,' among his intimates no one could have been more gay, witty, and natural. Though his acquaintances might find him cold, his friends knew well what a tender and generous soul shone in the thoughtful eyes. If he listened to a tale of sorrow coldly and critically almost, while others were commiserating the unfortunate, Condorcet was remedying the misfortune. Though he never could profess affection, he knew better than any man how to prove it; and if all his principles were stern, all his deeds were gentle. So quiet in his tastes that he had no use for riches, wholly without the arrogance and the blindness which distinguished his class, he had its every merit and not one of its faults; and he well deserved the title Voltaire gave him—'The man of the old chivalry and the old virtue.'

In 1770, when he was twenty-seven, he went with d'Alembert to stay at Ferney. Voltaire was delighted with him. Here was a man after his own heart, with his own hatred of oppression and fanaticism and his own zeal for humanity, with better chances of serving it! The Patriarch did not add, as he might have added, that this young Condorcet had a thousand virtues a Voltaire could never compass—that he was pure in life and hated a lie; that he was wholly without jealousy, without vanity, and without meanness. Caritat soon worshipped at the feet of a master of whom his friendship with d'Alembert had already proclaimed him a pupil, while Voltaire enlisted his guest's quiet, practical help for the rehabilitation of the Chevalier de la Barre, for the revision of the process of d'Étallonde; and honoured him by becoming his editor and assistant in the critical 'Commentary on Pascal' which Condorcet produced later.

Because his humility was the humility of a just mind and his modesty of the kind that scorns to cringe, Condorcet's admiration for his host did not blind him to his literary faults or make him meanly spare them; and while it was Condorcet who spoke in warm eulogy of his 'dear and illustrious chief as working not for his glory but for his cause, it was also Condorcet who deprecated that production of Voltaire's senility, 'Irene.' Sometimes the three friends would talk over the future of France—the two older men who had done much to mould that future and the young man who had much to do. 'You will see great days,' old Voltaire wrote afterwards to his guest; 'you will make them.'

The visit lasted a fortnight, and was a liberal education indeed.

Three years later, in 1773, Condorcet received the crown of his success as a mathematician and was made Perpetual Secretary of the Academy of Sciences, where he wrote *éloges* of the savants who had belonged to it, with the noble motto for ever in his mind, 'One owes to the dead only what is useful to the living—justice and truth.'

So far, Condorcet had been a mathematician alone. Knowledge might free and redeem the world—in time; but the time was long. Beneath that quiet exterior, palpitating through his leisurely, exact studies at the College of Navarre and the Scientific Academy, there throbbed in this man's breast a vaster and fiercer passion than any passion for learning—the passion for human-kind. Where did young Condorcet come by that ruling idea of his that opened to him a field of labour which he must till all his days, unremittingly, before the night cometh when no man can work—that idea which should steel him to endure, exulting, the cruellest torments of life and death—'the infinite perfectibility of human nature, the infinite augmentation of human happiness'?

The friend of d'Alembert was Condorcet, the geometrician; the friend of Turgot was Condorcet, the reformer.

X: CONDORCET: THE ARISTOCRAT

In August, 1774, Turgot was made Controller-General. He appointed Condorcet his Inspector of Coinage at a salary of 240*l*. a year, a payment which Condorcet never accepted. The pair had work to do, which only they could do, and do together. The vexed subject of Trade in Grain—'for a moment,' says Robinet, 'the whole question of the Revolution lay in this question of Grain'—incited them to fierce battle for what they took to be the cause of freedom against the cause of that well-meaning commonplace, Necker. Condorcet attacked Necker with a rare, fierce malignity, and wrote two stinging pamphlets on the subject which made him many enemies. But there were other reforms waiting the doing, less in importance then and greater in importance now. To curtail the advantages of the privileged classes, to open for commerce the rivers of central France, to abolish the slave trade, *Taille* and *Corvée*, *Vingtième* and *Gabelle*, and to make the nobility share in the taxation—these were the tasks into which this noble put his life and his soul. That every reform meant loss to himself, that all his interests were vested in the privileges he sought to destroy, that every human tie drew him towards the old order, makes his work for the new, more excellent than that of his fellow-workers. They had nothing to gain; Condorcet had everything to lose.

In May, 1776, a Queen of one-and-twenty demanded that 'le sieur Turgot fût chassé, même envoyé à la Bastille'; and, in part, she had her way, for her own ruin and that of France. Condorcet renounced his Inspectorship of Coinage; he would not serve under another master. Turgot's death in 1781 was the first great sorrow of his life. His other friend, d'Alembert, won for him a seat in the French Academy in 1782; and in the next year he too died. Condorcet tended him to the last, with that quiet and generous devotion which says little and does much. D'Alembert left to him the task of providing annuities for two old servants, and Condorcet accepted the obligation as a privilege, and fulfilled it scrupulously in his own poverty and ruin.

He was now not a little lonely. His relatives still resented his choice of a profession; his best friends were dead; the great Master of their party had preceded them. From 'social duties falsely so called' Caritat had long ago freed himself. He was three and forty years old, occupied in writing that 'Life of Turgot' which is a declaration of his own principles and policy, in contributing to the Encyclopædia, and in many public labours, when he first met Mademoiselle Sophie de

Grouchy.

If the supreme blessing of life be a happy marriage, then Condorcet was a fortunate man indeed. Mademoiselle was full twenty years younger than himself, very girlish in face and figure, with a bright cultivated mind, and a rare capacity for love and tenderness. He found in her what is uncommon even in happy marriages perhaps—his wife was also his friend. From the first she shared his work and his love for his fellow-men, approved of his sacrifices, and was true not only to him, but to his example of unselfish courage and unflinching devotion, to the end of her life.

For the moment—for what a brief moment!—their world looked smiling enough.

Condorcet abandoned himself to his happiness, with the deep passion of a strong man who has never wasted his heart in lighter feelings. For a dowry—so essential to a French marriage—he wholly forgot to stipulate. For the opinion of his friends, who considered a married geometrician as a sort of freak of Nature, he cared nothing; and when they saw his wife, and forgave him, their pardon was as little to him as their blame.

The two settled on the Quai de Conti in a house where Caritat had previously lived with his mother. At that Hôtel des Monnaies Sophie held her *salon* (*le foyer de la République*, men called it), where she received, with a youthful charm and grace, not only her husband's French political friends, but also Lord Stormont the English Ambassador, Wilkes, Garrick, Sterne, Hume, Robertson, Gibbon, Mackintosh, and Adam Smith.

Large and shy, with a little awkwardness even in his manner, it was not Condorcet but his wife who was socially successful. She was the one woman in a thousand who estimated social success at its low, just value, and was great in knowing her husband to be much greater.

Only two years after their marriage, in 1788, Condorcet entered the arena as one of the earliest and most noteworthy of all champions of Women's Rights. On the ground of their equal intelligence he claimed for them equal privileges with men, and ignored the very suggestion that their bodily weakness and inferiority are reproduced in their minds. He judged, in fact, all women from one woman. No nobler testimony can be borne to the intellect and character of the Marquise de Condorcet than to say that she deserved as an individual what her example made her husband think of her

X: CONDORCET: THE ARISTOCRAT

sex.

It is not a little curious to note that Condorcet, though so wholly faithful and happy himself in the relationship, thought the indissolubility of marriage an evil. In later years, he pleaded warmly for the condemnation of mercenary marriages by public opinion, as one of the best means of lessening the inequalities of wealth.

In 1790, the profound happiness of his wedded life was crowned by the birth of his only child, a daughter. Before that, the fierce whirlpool of politics had drawn him into it, and he had addressed the electors of the States-General and appeared publicly as the enemy of sacerdotalism and aristocracy, with all his gospel based on two great principles—the natural rights of man and the mutable nature of the constitutions which govern him. He was made member of the municipality of Paris, and in that, his first public function, flung the gauntlet before his caste and broke for ever with an order of which the smug selfishness was admirably typified by a Farmer-General who said to him, 'Why alter things? We are very comfortable.'

The fall of the Bastille, the insurrection of October, the journey of the Royal Family to Paris, he had watched with the calm of one who knows that such things must needs be, who realises the necessity of painful means to a glorious end. To the monarchy he was not at first opposed. If the King were but a man! But when in June, 1791, came the ignominious flight to Varennes, Condorcet rose in a fierce, still wrath and proclaimed the necessity for a Republic. 'The King has freed himself from us, we are freed from him,' said he. 'This flight enfranchises us from all our obligations.'

Nearly all the Marquis's friends broke with him, and he stood alone. Before his ripened views on royalty were fully known, it had been proposed that he should be the tutor of the Dauphin, and to Sophie that she should be the *gouvernante*. Husband and wife were in different places when the proposals were made; but, though they had never spoken with each other on the subject, they declined the offers almost in the same words. If Condorcet's friends misunderstood him and parted at the parting of the ways, his wife never did.

In 1791, he was elected member for Paris in the Legislative Assembly and became in quick succession its Secretary and its President. As its President, he presented to it his Educational Scheme, startlingly modern in its demands that education should be free and unsectarian.

By the order of the Assembly, in 1792, there was burnt in Paris an immense number of the brevets and patents of nobility — among them the patent of Jean Antoine Nicolas de Caritat, Marquis de Condorcet — at the very moment when at the bar of the tribune Condorcet himself demanded that the same measure should be adopted all over France. Not one dissentient voice was raised against the scheme; who, indeed, should dissent from it when a marquis proposed it? A few months later he was elected Member of the National Convention for the Department of Aisne, and the extremist of the Legislative Assembly found himself all too moderate for the Convention.

Then came the trial of the King.

There was never a time when Condorcet could be called either an orator or a leader of men. Though he had written most of its official addresses, he had appeared but little before the Legislative Assembly. Nervousness caused him always to read any speeches he did make, and a delicate voice robbed them of their eflFectiveness. His deeds and his character earned him a hearing and applause; and sometimes his complete self-devotion and the white heat of his enthusiasm discounted his manner and touched his hearers with something of his own deathless passion. But he was, as d'Alembert said, a volcano covered with snow, and that audience of his, coarse in fibre, mad for excitement, overwrought, uncontrolled, must needs see the mountain in flames, vomiting lava and death.

To be a great orator one must have in a supreme degree the qualities one's hearers have in a lesser degree. The thoughtful reason and the lofty ideals of Condorcet found little counterpart in the parliaments of the Revolution. A Marat or a Danton for us! Or a Fouquier-Tinville even, drunk with blood, with his wild hair flung back, and his words shaking with passion; but not this noble, with the high courage of his caste, his 'stoical Roman face,' his stern truthfulness, his unworldly enthusiasms. Worse than all, Condorcet never was for a cause, but always for a principle; and since he followed no party blindly, he was in turn abused by all.

He proved in his own history that to be a great demagogue it is essential to be without too fine a scrupulousness and the more delicate virtues; that successfully to lead the vulgar the first requisite is not to be too much of a gentleman.

Condorcet, although he had broken with monarchy as a possible form of government for France, had still no personal feeling against the monarch. Firmly convinced of his

culpability, he was equally convinced that the Convention was not legally competent to judge its King at all; and proposed that he should be tried by a tribunal chosen by the electors of the Departments of France. But to take the judging of its sovereign from the Convention was to take the prey whose blood he has tasted from the tiger. When the great moment came, Condorcet was at Auteuil; he hastened to Paris, and arrived at the Assembly a few moments before the King. What a strange contrast was this Marquis—serene in strong purpose, with his 'just mind justly fixed,' great in his compassion for his country and not without compassion for his King—to that poor Bourbon, 'who means well had he any fixed meaning,' and whom Condorcet himself described in an admirable but rarely quoted description as standing before his judges, 'uneasy, rather than frightened; courageous, but without dignity.'
On January 15, 1793, to the momentous question if the prisoner at the bar were guilty, Condorcet answered, 'Yes:' he had conspired against liberty. On the 17th and 18th the vote was taken on the nature of the punishment to be awarded. Consider the judgment-hall filled with the fierce faces and wild natures of men who, for centuries starved of their liberties, had drunk the first maddening draught of power. Consider that among them this noble alone represented a class they hated worse than they hated royalty itself, that if he had forsworn it, broken with it, denied it, he had still its high bearing, its maddening self-possession and self-control. We vote for death—shall you dare to know better? An Orleans sitteth and speaketh against his own kin; why not a noble, then, who owes him nothing? Condorcet rises in his place and pronounces for exile—the severest penalty in the penal code which is not death. 'The punishment of death is against my principles, and I shall not vote for it. I propose further that the decision of the Convention shall be ratified by an appeal to the people.'
On Saturday, January 19, 1793, the execution of the King having been fixed for the Monday, Condorcet implored his colleagues to neutralise the fatal effect of their decision on the other European Powers by abolishing the punishment of death altogether. With the Terror then struggling to the birth in her wild breast, one of the greatest children of his country begged for the suppression of that penalty as the most 'efficacious way of perfecting human-kind in destroying that leaning to ferocity which has long dishonoured it.

Punishments which admit of correction and repentance are the only ones fit for regenerated humanity.'

In the roar of that fierce storm of human passions, the quiet voice was unheeded, but not unheard. There were those who looked up at the speaker, and remembered his words—for his ruin. How far, up to this point, Condorcet realised his danger is hard to say. A Louis, with the fatal blindness of kingship, might believe to the last that his person really *was* inviolable, that from the tumbril itself loyal hands would deliver his majesty from the insult of a malefactor's death. But a Condorcet?

The immediate result of his part in the King's trial was that his name was struck from the roll of the Academies of St. Petersburg and Berlin. That insult touched him so little that there is not a single allusion to it in his writings.

In the month succeeding the King's death, a Commission of nine members of the Convention, of whom Condorcet was one, laid before it their project for the New Constitution of the Year II, to which Condorcet had written an elaborate Preface. The project was not taken. Hérault de Séchelles made a new one. In his bold and scathing criticism upon it—his 'Appeal to the French Citizens on the Project of the New Constitution'— Condorcet signed his own condemnation.

On July 8,1793, Chabot denounced that 'Appeal' at the Convention. This ex-Marquis, he said, is 'a coward, a scoundrel, and an Academician.' 'He pretends that his Constitution is better than yours. that primary assemblies ought to be accepted, *therefore* I propose that he ought to be arrested and brought to the bar.' On the strength of this logical reasoning and without evidence of any kind against him, the Convention decreed that Condorcet's papers should be sealed and that he should be put under arrest and on the list of those who were to be tried before the Revolutionary Tribunal on the coming third of October. He was further condemned in his absence and declared to be *hors la loi*.

If it is doubtful whether Condorcet realised the probable effect of his opinion and vote in the matter of the King's trial, he had realised to the full the jeopardy in which the 'Appeal' would place him. But he looked now, as he had looked always, not to the effect his deeds might have on his own destiny, but to their effect on the destiny of the race. If the unit could but do his part for the mass, then, having done it, he must be content to be trampled under its feet, happy, if on his dead body some might rise and catch a glimpse of a Promised Land.

X: CONDORCET: THE ARISTOCRAT

But yet he must save himself if he could.

For seven years, through storms of which the story still shakes men's souls, he had known in his own home, first on the Quai de Conti and then in the Rue de Lille, the deep, calm joys of his happy marriage. When the troubles of life come only from without, through the fiercest of such troubles man and wife may be happy still. It is those evils alone which rise from their own characters which can wholly destroy the beauty of life. In the serene tenderness of the woman who kept for ever, it is said, some of the virgin freshness of the girl, who united to strength gentleness, and to courage quietness, who was at once modest and clever, simple and intelligent, Condorcet was given a rich share of the best earth has to offer.

Their *salon*, of course, was no more. The beating of the pitiless storm had driven their Englishmen to covert in happier England. But it is only when one is discontented with one's relatives that there is crying need of acquaintances, These two still had each other and their child, Condorcet had much to lose.

To go to the Rue de Lille would be courting death. He escaped first to his country home at Auteuil. From there, two friendly doctors took him to a house in the Rue Servandoni, belonging to Madame Vernet, the widow of the sculptor, and asked her to shelter a proscribed man. She only inquired if he was good and virtuous. When they answered, 'Yes,' she consented at once. 'Do not lose a moment, you can tell me about him later.' Regarding the value of the works of her husband there have been many opinions, but as to the value of her work there can be only one. Perfectly aware that she was endangering her life for a fugitive whom she had never seen, and who had not the slightest claim upon her generosity, she sheltered him for nine months, providing him all the time with every necessary of life and without the smallest hope of repayment. When he did leave her at last, he had to steal away from her self-sacrificing care by a subterfuge, like a thief. Strong, simple and energetic, high in courage and devotion, Madame Vernet is one of the unsung heroines of history.

Condorcet's condition was destitute indeed As an outlaw all his money had been seized. For himself that might have been bearable; even to the fate he foresaw too clearly he could be indifferent—for himself. One Sarret, to whom Madame Vernet was privately married and who lived in the house, speaks of the fugitive's gentleness, patience, and resignation. He had given to his country his talents, his time, his fortune, his rank;

and when she turned and rent him, he had for her nothing but compassion and the strong hope of a day that would dawn upon her clear and fair, after the storm was past.

But in the knowledge that he had brought ruin and disgrace on what he loved best in the world, Condorcet sounded one of the great deeps of human suffering. As the wife of an outlaw, Madame de Condorcet was not only penniless, but could not even sleep in the capital. Wholly dependent on her was her little girl of three years old, a young sister, and an old governess. She was herself still young and brought up in a class unused to work, in the sense of work to make money, for generations. But there was in her soul the great courage of a great love. The talents which had once charmed her *salon* she now turned to a means of livelihood. When her house at Auteuil was invaded by Republican soldiers, Madame softened their hearts and earned a pittance by taking their portraits. Twice a week, disguised as a peasant, she came on foot from Auteuil to Paris, passed through the gates with the fierce crowds thronging to the executions in the Place de la Révolution, and by painting miniatures of the condemned in the prisons, of proscribed men lying hidden in strange retreats, or of middle-class citizens, made enough to support her little household. Then, sometimes, she would creep to the Rue Servandoni, and for a few minutes forget parting, death, and the terrors of the unknown future, in her husband's arms. He might well write, as he did write but a little while before he died, that even then he was not all unhappy—he had served his country and had had her heart.

He spent the long days of his hiding almost entirely in writing. He began by an exposition of his principles and conduct during the Revolution, and gave an account of his whole public career. He was writing it when, on October 3, 1793, he was tried, in his absence, before the Revolutionary Tribunal, with Vergniaud, Brissot, and others, accused of conspiring against the unity of the Republic, declared an emigrant, and condemned to death.

On the 31st of the same month came the fall of the Girondins. Though not himself a Girondin they had been once his friends, and in their ruin he saw the immediate presage of his own; and his own meant that also of Madame Vernet. He went to her at once. 'The law is clear; if I am discovered here you will die as I shall. I am *hors la loi*; I cannot remain here longer.' She answered that though he might be *hors la loi* he was not outside the law of humanity; and bade him stay where he was.

X: CONDORCET: THE ARISTOCRAT

His wife, in her peasant's dress, came to him then for one of those brief moments, stolen from Heaven. She knew him well. That 'Justification' of his conduct, his Apologia, that looking back on deeds and sacrifices meant to bring the Golden Age to men and which *had* brought, or so it seemed, the hell of the Terror—this was no fit work for him now. Look ahead! Look on to that new country which your pure patriotism and your self-devotion,—ay, and this Terror itself— shall have helped to make—that warless world of equal rights and ever widening knowledge, the beautiful dream of a sinless and sorrowless earth, which may yet be realised, in part.

On the manuscript of the 'Justification' there is written in her hand '*Left at my request to write the History of the Progress of the Human Mind.*'

In the very shadow of death, Condorcet told the story of men's advance toward life, of the evolution of their understanding from the earliest times until now. Calm, just, and serene, with not an intemperate line, not an angry thought, the 'Progress' reads as if it had been written by some tranquil philosopher who had seen his plan for man's redemption adopted, and had received for his labour honours, peace, and competence. Its fault, indeed, is its too sanguine idealism. Condorcet, like many enthusiasts, thought his own way of salvation for man the only way; he believed his own magnificent dream to be the only possible Utopia.

Beneath the guillotine and in social convulsions for which history has no parallel, he looked through and past them, in that last great chapter, in the exalted spirit of noble prophecy, to that Golden Age which *must* surely come!

But 'The Progress of the Human Mind' is something more than a splendid hope, more than the greatest and most famous of its author's works. It bears highest testimony to the character of him who in the supreme hour of his individual life could thus forget himself, and in the midst of personal ruin, foresee with exultant joy the salvation of the race.

It remains for ever among the masterpieces which men cannot afford to forget.

During his hiding Condorcet also wrote 'The Letter of Junius to William Pitt' in which he expresses his aversion to Pitt, and an essay, never printed, 'On the Physical Degradation of the Royal Races.' He also planned a universal philosophical language.

In December, 1793, he wrote 'The Letter of a Polish Exile in Siberia to his Wife'—a poem in which another exile bade farewell to the woman he loved.

The death-shadows were creeping closer now.

In March, 1794, he finished 'The Progress of the Human Mind.' But before that he had decided to leave Madame Vernet; her danger was too great. Early in January he had begun writing his last wishes, the 'Advice of a Proscribed Father to his Daughter.' The little girl was the child of too deep a love not to be infinitely dear. To what was he leaving her? Throughout these cruel months, the last drop in his cup of bitterness had been the strong conviction that his wife would share his own fate, was doomed, like himself, to the guillotine. 'If my daughter is destined to lose everything,' — even to himself he could not frame the dread thought in plainer words. But if even that thing must be, then he left Madame Vernet the guardian of his child, begging that she might have a liberal education which would help her to earn her own livelihood, and, in particular, that she might learn English, so that if need came she could seek the help of her mother's English friends.

To the little girl herself he left words of calm and beautiful counsel, which are in themselves a possession. Some of that 'light that never was on sea or land' lies surely on those tender and gracious lines, something of the serene illumination that shines from a dying face.

In the early morning of April 5, 1794, the Marquis de Condorcet laid down his pen for the last time.

At ten o'clock on that day he slipped out of the house in the Rue Servandoni, unknown to Madame Vernet, and in spite of the passionate protests of Sarret, her husband, who followed him out into the street, praying him to return. Condorcet was in his usual disguise; many months' confinement indoors, and the old weakness in his limbs, made walking a difficulty. He was at the door almost of the fatal prisons of the Carmes and the Luxembourg; but no persuasions could make him return. He had heard rumours of a domiciliary visit to be made immediately to Madame Vernet's house and, were he found there, she *must* be ruined. Sarret implored in vain. The fugitive reached the Maine barrier in safety and turned in the direction of Fontenay-aux-Roses. At every step his pain and difficulty in walking increased. But at three o'clock in the afternoon he safely reached the country house of his old friends, the Suards.

Madame Suard may be remembered as the very enthusiastic and vivacious little lady who once visited Voltaire, who has left behind her entertaining 'Letters,' and who has recorded Voltaire's warm love and admiration for her friend Condorcet. 'Our dear and good Condorcet,' Madame Suard had called him. She and her husband (who was a well-known journalist and wit) had been his intimate friends in prosperity; how could he do better than come to them in his need?

It must in justice be said of the Suards that the accounts of their conduct are confused. But the generally accepted, as well as the most probable, story does not redound to their credit. True, they had many excuses; but there has never been any act of treachery for which the treacherous have not been able to adduce a plausible reason.

Condorcet asked for one night's lodging, and M. Suard replied that such hospitality would be quite as dangerous for Condorcet himself as for them. Still, they could give him money, some ointment for a chafed leg due to his long walk, and a copy of Horace—to amuse his leisure! Further, we will not lock our garden-gate to-night so that in case of urgent need you can make use of it! With this, they sent him away. Madame Vernet, searching for him in that neighbourhood a little while after, declared that she tried the garden-gate and found it rusty and immovable. Her own door, in lawless Paris, was open night and day that, if he should return to her, she should not fail him. Whether he attempted to make use of the Suards' timid hospitality is not known. One would think of Condorcet that he did not.

The day of April 6 he spent in sufferings and privations which can only be guessed.

On April 7, a tall man, gaunt and famished, with a wound in his leg, went into an inn of Clamart and asked for an omelette. Mine host, looking at him suspiciously, inquired how many eggs he would have in his omelette. The Marquis, with no kind of idea of the number of eggs a working-man, or any man for that matter, expects in his omelette, said a dozen. M. Crépinet, the innkeeper, was a shrewd person as well as one of the municipals of the Commune. A queer workman this! Your name? Peter Simon, was the answer. Papers? I have none. Occupation? Well, on the spur of the moment, a carpenter. His hands, whose only tool had been a pen, gave him the lie. Crépinet, pleased with his own sharpness, had this strange carpenter arrested and marched toward Bourg-la-Reine.

How in these supreme moments Condorcet felt and acted, is not on record. But in the great crises men unconsciously produce that character which they have formed in the trivial

round of daily life, and he who would be great at great moments must be a great character by his own fireside and in the dull routine of his ordinary work. The strong, quiet Condorcet was surely strong and quiet still—'the victim of his foes,' as he had said, 'but never their instrument or their dupe.' On that weary way, a compassionate vine-dresser took pity on his limping condition, and lent him a horse.
On the morning of April 8, 1794, when the jailor of the prison of Bourg-la-Keine came to hand over the new prisoner to the *gendarmes* who had arrived to take him to Paris, the Marquis de Condorcet was found dead in his cell. With a powerful preparation of opium and stramonium prepared by his friend Cabanis, the celebrated physician, and which Condorcet had long carried about with him in his ring, he had 'cheated the guillotine.' It was remembered afterwards, that when he left the Suards' house, he had turned saying, 'If I have one night before me, I fear no man; but I will not be taken to Paris.'
That he who gave his life to the people Revolutionist have defrauded them, as it were, of his death strikes the one discord in the clear harmony of this true soul.
Better that a Condorcet, like many a lesser man, should have mounted the guillotine as a king mounts his throne, proud to die for the cause for which he had lived, and hearing through the blasphemy and the execrations of the rabble below, the far-off music of a free and happy people.
For many months the woman who loved him had no news of his death. She hoped against hope that he had escaped, and was in safety in Switzerland. To support her little household she took a fine-linen shop in the Rue St. Honoré, and in the *entresol* set up her little studio where she continued her portrait-painting.
In January, 1794, for the good and safety of their child, she had heroically petitioned the municipality for a divorce from her husband, and obtained it—six weeks after his death. When the certain news of that death reached her, both her health and her strong heart faltered. But Doctor Cabanis, who afterwards married her young sister, saved her—for further effort and longer work.
Full of courage and resignation she rose up again, wrote a preface to 'The Progress of the Human Mind,' educated her child, and when in 1795 some of her fortune was restored, immediately began paying the pensions which d'Alembert had asked Condorcet to give his old servants.
In later days she had a little *salon* in Paris, saw her daughter

X: CONDORCET: THE ARISTOCRAT

happily married, and died in 1822. In every stupendous change which France experienced between the fall of Robespierre and the death of Napoleon Bonaparte, she remained faithful to the principles to which her husband had devoted his genius and his life.

Through all, the Marquise de Condorcet had been, and had counted herself, a happy woman. Wrung with such sorrows as do not fall to the lot of many of her sex, she had had a blessing which is the portion of far fewer of them; she had inspired a great devotion, and had been worthy of it.

To Condorcet is meted now in some sort the same judgment as was meted to him in life.

Since he never gave himself blindly to any one faction, all factions have distrusted and condemned him. To the Royalist he is a Revolutionist; to the Revolutionist he is an aristocrat. The thinker cannot forgive him that his thought led him to deeds and words; the man of action cannot forget that he was thinker and dreamer to the end. While the Church can never pardon his persistent hostility to theology, his vehement opposition to Roman Catholicism, as the religion 'where a few rogues make many dupes,' the unbeliever is impatient with his serene faith in human kind, his unshattered trust in the goodness, not of God, but of man.

Far in advance of his time—in some respects of our time too—in his views on the rights of men and of women, on the education of children, and in his steady abhorrence of all limitation of what Voltaire called 'the noble liberty of thinking,' he is still condemned for an unpractical idealism, and for his passionate conviction that all errors are the fruit of bad laws.

But he at least stands out clearly to any impartial observer as one of the very few whose lofty disinterestedness came unscorched through the fire of the Terror.

In private life, stern to duty and yet tenderer than any woman in his quiet, deep affections, patient and strong with the fine endurance of steel and with the capacity (that capacity which is as rare as genius) for the highest form of human love, he showed a great character beside which even his great intellect seems a small thing and a mean.

In the breadth and the generosity of his self-sacrifice for the public good, he remains for ever one of the noblest, not only of the Friends of Voltaire, but of the sons of France.

CPSIA information can be obtained
at www.ICGtesting.com
Printed in the USA
LVHW091342160121
676557LV00043B/215